Motivating for Change

How to Manage Employee Stress

■

NICOLA PHILLIPS

the Institute of Management

F O U N D A T I O N

PITMAN
PUBLISHING

PITMAN PUBLISHING
128 Long Acre, London WC2E 9AN

A Division of Pearson Professional Limited

First published in Great Britain 1995

© Nicola Phillips 1995

British Library Cataloguing in Publication Data
A CIP catalogue record for this book can be obtained
from the British Library

ISBN 0 273 61176 3

1 3 5 7 9 10 8 6 4 2

Typeset by Northern Phototypesetting Co. Ltd, Bolton
Printed and bound in Great Britain by
Bell and Bain Ltd, Glasgow

*The Publishers' policy is to use paper manufactured
from sustainable forests.*

Contents

■

COUNSELLING IN CONTEXT

APPENDICES

Acknowledgements

■

Special thanks to Evelyn Lee Barber for trusting me, and for support on numerous risky projects. Penny Jaques provided a source of perception and understanding that ensured my personal growth and development. Thanks to my family, particularly Joyce, who started me down the counselling road, and Alex and Cheryl whose stability has ensured that I stayed on the road. Special thanks are reserved for Lauren and Peter who support and care for me in their different ways and have provided the couch on several occasions for me ...

ix

The most conspicuous mark of the moral level of any community is the value it sets on human personality

B. H. STREETER

Introduction:
Changing work patterns and values

■

The current commercial and economic climate has resulted in some major changes within organisations. Many of these changes have been reactive, and have necessarily involved unpleasant duties. Consolidation and flattening within an organisation to deal with external and internal changes mean that the company is unable to provide frequent and speedy moves both across and up the company. People are remaining, or will have to remain, in the same role for a great deal longer, with fewer opportunities for movement. The outcome of this is a potentially demotivated workforce, unless managers find different ways of developing their staff other than through money or promotion.

In the leaner, 'meaner' environment of the nineties and beyond, the concept of 'doing more with less', in terms of employees, has created an impetus to acquire the interpersonal skills that will retain and motivate staff needed to create competitive advantage.

Where are the interpersonal skills to retain and motivate staff?

What will the manager of the future be expected to do? Most people agree that tomorrow's worker, unfettered by yesterday's constraints of hierarchy and job boundaries, will be far more independent and self-directed than today's. Will such a worker even need managing in today's accepted sense of the word? Self-management has always existed, but previously it meant taking care of yourself while you followed the leader. In the future, self-management will mean acting as a stakeholder in the task at hand. This does not mean there is no role for a manager; what it means is there is a role for a guide, co-ordinator and facilitator. To move things on at an appropriate speed, tomorrow's managers will need to provide information for their workers, and facilitate their decision making. This will mean more of a role for the manager in talking through situations to enable people to come to and commit to their decisions; they will need to be able to support their workers when the going gets tough, but not take over. They will need to be more observant of situations and intuitive about when to step in and when to let go.

Do today's managers use these skills? Do they understand them?

This book looks at counselling skills as a medium for stimulating staff performance. Managers need to become facilitators rather than commanders; leading by coaching, counselling and encouragement for continuous improvement. This is not a process that will happen on its own, but one that needs to be led and focused by management. In order to 'do more with less', and renew the flagging motivation of middle and

Managers need to be concerned with potential not power.

junior managers, a fundamental change in the way people manage and motivate their departments is required. Managers need to be concerned with *potential* not power; releasing and channelling all the abilities and resources in their groups.

This book examines the skills and knowledge required to energise and encourage the workforce and take them forward. These include those skills necessary to instigate, facilitate and manage pressure productively.

The three main aims of this book are:

- to give a background to the nature and application of counselling in the workplace of the future;
- to identify situations and opportunities where counselling can be used to manage the process of change, increasing motivation and performance; and
- to suggest ways of maximising the potential of managers, teams and individuals in a changing environment, using counselling skills.

Every counselling situation involves both counsellor and client. Personal growth is directly related to the development of the relationship between them. Hopefully, this book will contribute towards understanding this relationship.

Counselling has never been the 'soft' option that many managers think it is. Indeed, it is the lack of those challenging skills required for counselling that has created the bulk of management problems. Developing and challenging performance are the key skills for the successful manager of the future.

The most that we can hope to do is to train every individual to realise all his potentialities and become completely himself.

ALDOUS HUXLEY

1

Counselling – What is it?

Summary

In this chapter, we look at some of the fundamental issues of counselling. If we are saying that the skill of counselling is central to the activities of a manager, it is therefore crucial that every manager understands what counselling is, is not, and when and how to use it.

Counselling in management means:

- **being non-directive**
- **being non-judgmental**
- **empathy**
- **confidentiality**
- **helping to release tension**
- **helping to release creative energy**
- **the individual wants it**
- **ownership of the problem stays with the 'individual'.**

Counselling in management does *not* mean:

- **sympathy**
- **advice**
- **giving or forcing solutions**
- **a 'soft' option**

The skills of counselling are the skills of creating and maintaining good human relationships. As such, they are of prime importance to all managers.

What do we mean by counselling?

Counselling is one of the most productive tools a manager can use. Why?

Because it involves recognising the importance of a member of staff by spending time listening to them. There are few things as motivating to people as the thought that someone is interested in them. We all need approval and seek it in varying ways. Giving recognition to staff by giving them time, is the most powerful and least used motivator. It is *not* a soft option, and is a great deal more difficult than telling someone what to do and how to do it. That demands few skills and has a very short-term effect. It is unlikely to solve an underlying problem, and will not guarantee the recipient's commitment to the solution.

The purpose of counselling is *not to tell people what to do, but to help them explore and understand the situation they are in*. Only when they have done this can they deal with the situation.

If management is about developing staff to their full potential in order to work at their most productive for themselves and the organisation, then counselling is a crucial skill for the manager.

Counselling is a much abused word. It can mean anything from a quick word in the corridor to a series of regular hour long sessions. In terms of counselling in the workplace, it will probably mean both of these and some other activities in between. It can be done to varying degrees by line management, functional managers, personnel staff, or external staff. The appropriate person will vary with the situation and individual. Even if, as a manager, you never officially 'counsel' anyone, it is vital that you understand what counselling is, and what it can do. On reading about counselling, you may find you do a lot of it, but do not call it counselling. It is therefore important to understand what it is you have been trying to do, and whether you might improve on your methods. It is necessary to accept that counselling is not just something that social workers and therapists do, but an indispensable part of the manager's routine.

Among all the definitions of counselling, some themes persist. Counselling is seen as:

'the process ... of giving ... help to persons suffering from fully conscious conflicts.'

'a two person situation in which one person ... is helped to adjust ... to himself and to his environment.'

'a face to face relationship in which ... [one person] ... is consciously attempting by verbal means to assist another person to modify emotional attitudes which are socially maladjusted.'

'a learning oriented process ... in which a counsellor ... seeks to assist [the other person] ... to learn more about himself ... [and to develop] ... more realistic ... goals [so] that [he] may become a happier and more productive member of his society.'

'a personal and dynamic relationship between two people ... with mutual consideration for each other ... to the end that [one] is aided to a self-determined resolution of his problem.'

'a counsellor helps [the other] to marshal his own resources ... to achieve the optimum adjustment of which he is capable.'

'a permissive relationship which allows [the counsellee] to gain an understanding of himself [and so] take positive steps.'

'a conversation or series of conversations between two persons ... to resolve the conflicts, reduce the anxiety and/or modify ...

3

response. Counselling is obviously a learning situation.'

'Talking, listening, sharing, caring, complex, asking the right questions and allowing the person to come up with solutions to what are perceived as problems.'

'To get people to look at things from a different angle/perspective.'

So, what is counselling?

4

> **Counselling is a way of responding and relating to someone so that they feel clearer about what is concerning them. They then feel better able to help themselves and make their own decisions. It helps them to talk about, and work out what their feelings are, before taking any action. It is this *exploration and understanding, before action*, which is special about counselling.**

> **There are many definitions of counselling: all of them agree on the basic principle that *counselling is about helping people to help themselves*.**

This is important, because most of us have difficulty, to a greater or lesser degree, in taking responsibility for our own lives. **The concept of personal responsibility is at the heart of the counselling process**. Taking responsibility demands a high level of self-awareness. This means that you have to understand yourself, and your reasons for behaving in a particular way in particular situations. This understanding is one of the outcomes of the counselling process. You need this understanding of why you do things before you can change the behaviour.

There is a school of thought, called behavioural counselling, which uses reward as a means of acquiring or strengthening behaviour, and this will sometimes achieve a change. However, because you do not know why you behaved that way in the first place, it is very probable that the same behaviour you have tried to change will reoccur. Also, because the reward is external and specific, the results are specific to that piece of behaviour.

Here is an example of a manager trying to help a team member who was finding it very difficult to control team meetings:

Team member: I don't know what I'm doing wrong, but I never seem to be able to get through all the agenda items. When a discussion starts, I don't know how, but it seems to take over.

Manager: You mustn't let them take control. You have to let them know who is running the meeting. What you have to do is strictly monitor the agenda, time discussions and keep strictly to the allotted time and subjects. By doing this, you will regain control of the meetings.

The team member is clearly at a loss to know what takes the meetings 'out of control'. The advice his manager gives him is very sound, but does not help him understand what is going wrong. If he does not know what it is about meetings that makes him lose control, any instant solutions will be short lived. So it is not that the advice is incorrect, it is like curing the symptoms of a disease without knowing the cause – the chances are you may not cure it, or it may reoccur. If, however, you can understand the reasons for acting in a particular way in particular situations, the potential for change, and permanent change is far greater.

> **With a broader understanding of yourself, you can react far more effectively to internal and external forces in order to achieve goals and meet needs.**

For the purposes of this book, we will be viewing counselling as a 'repertoire of skills', used to establish and maintain a supportive relationship. This relationship is essentially **'non-directive'** and aimed at **'empowering'** the person. This means that it does not involve the counsellor telling the individual what to do, but rather helping the person come to an understanding of their situation, and devising their own solutions about what they will do.

> **The counsellor's skills include those of forming relationships, and skills focused on helping the person to change specific aspects of their thinking, feeling and behaviour.**

Counselling is not only about helping people through difficult situations, it is about developing capabilities and releasing creative energies. It is a very positive and productive action, rather than an activity that goes on when people are in trouble. This is a side of counselling that is rarely emphasised, and it is one that has considerable significance for the manager.

You may want to use counselling to help someone realise talents and skills you have spotted but they have not. For example, you may have someone on your team who you feel has the potential to take on a new post with more responsibilities. They may feel unable to do this. Telling them will not make them feel able to do it. It is not enough to say to someone that they are wonderful; they have to realise it, understand it, and accept it themselves. This acceptance can be achieved through the counselling process.

Counselling also helps release tension, which can block a person's ability to create and function normally. This is possibly the most frequent occasion when a manager will feel it appropriate to counsel. (See the example below.)

Case study

Janet, an editor in a publishing company, was very bright, vivacious and full of ideas. She was always happy to work on her own initiative, and set her own goals and deadlines. She was extremely successful, and was left to manage on her own. When she had her first child, she took three months off and came back to work. At first no one seemed to notice any difference in her work. However, after about three weeks, her manager noticed that she was being very abrupt with her team, and was unable to give them instructions or guidance in their work.

When the manager talked to Janet about it, she lost her temper and said that a huge pile of work had accumulated while she was away and how was she supposed to cope with the volume of work with such an undisciplined team? This was not the kind of outburst that her manager would have associated with Janet.

She broached the subject with Janet, who said that everything felt too much for her. They agreed that much of Janet's anger was due to her perceived inability to function at her previous level, without allowing for the extra, unusual pressure that Janet was under because of the baby.

After a counselling session, they agreed that Janet was not functioning to her normal level because of external circumstances, and she needed some support to help her 're-entry' to work. The manager agreed to provide Janet with some structure, and give Janet deadlines instead of Janet setting them herself. They agreed to review the situation in six months.

At the end of that time, Janet was beginning to function almost to her normal level, and they agreed that Janet could now begin to put back her own structures. Within a year, Janet was working on her own, and producing her normal standard of work.

What Janet had needed was someone to help her identify what was going wrong, and help her sort out a means of dealing with it. Her manager gave her the time and the 'space', and was rewarded with a fully functioning member of staff.

Counselling has a role to play in facilitating change and adapting to change. For example, redundancy, career change, personal circumstances, role change are all times when counselling might prove a useful tool for the manager. This role can be twofold: to help someone adjust to a change, and also to help support and maintain the change.

Having established how vital counselling is to the manager, why is it such a neglected skill?

Why is counselling neglected?

Let's look at some of the myths and misconceptions that surround counselling:

- it takes too long
- I don't have time for all that nonsense
- fear of stigma – am I ill?
- cultural fear of discussing personal issues
- nobody's business but my own
- I have to work it out on my own
- how will others see me?

- will it affect my promotion prospects?
- only wimps (or women) need to talk things through
- will it change me?
- will it make me talk about things I don't want to talk about?

These are all things people actually have said when faced with the counselling process. These thoughts come from managers and staff members, and seem to fall into three major categories:

1 It is a lengthy and time-consuming process.
2 It is culturally 'not OK'.
3 They do not know the outcome and effects of the process at the outset.

Let's look at these categories individually.

9

Argument

That it is a lengthy and time-consuming process:
- It takes too long
- I don't have time for all that nonsense.

Response

This is a 'How long is a piece of string?' question. It also begs the question 'What will be the effect of you doing nothing?'
It need not be a lengthy process. Sometimes all people need is a bit of 'space', and the time to verbalise their situation to clear their heads and enable them to act. This could be anything from five minutes to five weeks. Sometimes just *knowing* that there is someone you can freely talk to is enough.

All managers should be able to provide this forum for talking for their staff. This is a counselling skill. The level to which they develop the forum is down to each individual manager. However, this forum does not appear automatically, nor does it become yours with the title of 'manager'. You have to create an environment that encourages people to speak freely. Once this is established, the time will vary with each situation.

Some managers say that they are approachable, that their door is always open and people can always talk to them. The need to announce this, gives the lie to the statements. Very few managers can have their door always open: this is unrealistic and, in today's open-plan office, with fast moving teams, the manager may not even have an office. However, managers still need to be perceived as having 'an open door', metaphorically or otherwise. So when a member of staff comes along and finds the door closed on more than one occasion, that person will not feel able to be honest with that manager, as the manager has not been honest with them. It is not enough to tell people of your intentions. In order for people to believe them, they have to experience them in practice. This is part of the trusting, respecting relationship which is central to both management and counselling.

Argument	*Response*
That it is culturally 'not OK'. This summarises what is probably the largest group of reactions. It covers thoughts like:	The British do not like the idea of talking about themselves to someone else. We see it as being weak and self-indulgent. Physical problems are OK to discuss, but, somehow, we feel that if we have a personal problem we should be able to deal with it ourselves, and we have no right even to perceive it as a problem. This attitude can lead to an apparent and perceived lack of concern by managers for their staff. If you ask someone who they like having as a manager, or ask

- nobody's business but my own
- I have to work it out on my own
- will it affect my promotion prospects?
- only wimps (or women) need to talk things through
- will it change me?

- will it make me talk about things I don't want to talk about?
- will it change other people's views about me?
- I should be able to work this through myself. I *can't* need counselling.

yourself who you have liked having as a manager, you will find that the people you respect the most are not just those who achieve their work targets, but those who have done so by involving and listening to their staff.

In order for people to believe that talking to their manager about a problem will not damage their promotion prospects, they have to experience this as being true. If that is not something the manager can promise, he would do better to say so to the staff member. This would leave the responsibility for the problem with the staff member, but leave the staff/manager relationship enhanced by an honest response.

This is part of setting realistic boundaries to work relationships. There are limits imposed on the relationship by the organisation, by the staff member and by you as the potential counsellor. An essential part of counselling is the setting of, and keeping to, boundaries. Everyone needs to know how far they can go, and what they can and can't do. This stating of boundaries creates part of the security that is vital to strong, honest and productive relationships. Without this security, people will not feel 'safe' to discuss anything. Saying 'No' and referring people on are all part of the boundary setting. (The actual mechanics of boundary setting and contracting are dealt with in detail in Chapter 4.)

Giving a member of staff time and space to talk is one of the most fundamental roles of the manager. Giving time and valuing the member of staff is the easiest way to motivate people, yet it is the least used motivator – in fact, it is generally neglected. This is partly to do with a cultural perception of it

11

being weak to talk , but is also connected with a fear of invading other people's privacy. This is, to a degree, a fear of someone invading our own privacy, but we put our own fears onto the person. We have to separate what is *our* fear, and what is the individual's (see Chapter 8).

Argument	*Response*
That they do not know the outcome and effects of the process at the outset: ■ will it affect my promotion prospects? ■ will it change me? ■ will it make me talk about things I don't want to talk about?	There may be a fear that talking about a subject will bring people face to face with details about themselves that are unpleasant, or that they do not want to acknowledge. Therefore, counselling might enable them to talk about things they don't want to talk about and it might change their behaviour.

The fundamental detail to remember here is that **counselling**, by its very nature, **is a voluntary activity**. No one can 'make' anyone get involved in counselling. It has to be something the person wants to do, as it is they who have to take the responsibility. So, for example, it may not be a 'pleasant' experience for a person to come face to face with the fact that they need to control other people, or that they are perceived by their staff to be bossy and dictatorial. However, without the person's acceptance of the situation, no change can come about. As a manager, you run the risk of long-term damage within the team, and a reduction in work efficiency, if you avoid dealing with conflict.

An important issue to raise here is the limit of the 'manager as counsellor' role. This is discussed fully in Chapter 4, but it is important to say here that any counselling the manager does at work has a limitation placed on it by virtue of the manager's position and their skills. It is *not* the manager's place to indulge in amateur psychotherapy.

So, having looked at some of the issues of counselling, what are the principles of counselling itself?

The principles of counselling

There are four underlying tenets/principles of counselling:

First principle   **1**

That it is **real**, and not rooted in fantasy, and is about helping to deal with reality.

Second principle   **2**

That it demands **empathy**, which is the ability to understand someone else's frame of reference. This means being able to interpret another's tone of voice and vocabulary, **as they are meant by that person**. This obviously demands very good listening and observation skills, and an ability to understand the other person's feelings, even when they are badly expressed. Sympathy is a very different feeling, and in terms of moving people on, is a passive, unproductive emotion. Empathy, by contrast, is a complex and active emotion which involves both the counsellor and person. It can be defined as feeling *with* someone as opposed to feeling *for* someone. It means getting into someone else's head whilst staying in your own. Understanding someone else's framework, and exactly what they mean when they use particular words or phrases, and not imposing your personal interpretation.

Because understanding empathy is such a fundamental part of the counselling process, it might be helpful to illustrate the difference between empathy and sympathy with an example:

Individual: I'm terrified about doing that presentation tomorrow.

Counsellor: Oh dear, I know just how that feels. Don't worry, you'll be OK. (*Sympathetic*)

Counsellor: What is it that makes you feel so nervous? (*Empathic*)

Third principle   **3**

That it demands **acceptance** of the person and situation without judgement. This means that whatever feelings, reactions or sentiments the person expresses, the counsellor will not pass judgement on them, but put them into the context of the person and situation. This is one of the most difficult principles of counselling to adhere to, as it asks the counsellor to put aside what may be very deeply held beliefs and values for the length of the consultation. Without this acceptance, however, the person will not feel secure enough to disclose their deeply held beliefs and values, for fear of disapproval. Without this acceptance, there can be no empathy, and therefore no true understanding of the person's needs, fears and hopes.

Fourth principle   **4**

That the counsellor must be able to **'let go'**. This means allowing the person to identify, explore and make their *own* decisions about their situation. Again a difficult task for the counsellor, since their desire is to help the person, and it frequently seems easier to tell them what to do, particularly if they ask! (This is largely to do with the counsellor's motivation to counsel, and is discussed more fully in Chapter 8.) The aim of counselling is to enable the person to

14

be aware of, feel in control of, and take responsibility for, their particular situation. This is called 'owning' the problem or situation. This means that the situation belongs to the person, and it is the counsellor's role to help them gain and maintain ownership. One of the most important roles for a counsellor is that of an objective observer, who can see things the person cannot, because they are outside the situation. As soon as a counsellor loses this objectivity, they will be unable to help the person. Having helped the person to own the situation, the control over what happens in the situation remains with the person. Without this ownership, the control of the situation will pass to the counsellor, which will not in any way help the person. It is this 'letting go' which stops the counsellor feeling overwhelmed and 'involved' with the person.

15

This particular tenet of 'letting go' may be an issue for managers who are promoted because they are dynamic and forceful. If you feel that you need to be very directive, you need to assess whether the situation genuinely demands a directive approach (and many do), or whether it is you who demands a directive approach. Neither of these are counselling. Advice is directive and is not counselling. Giving advice implies you know more than the person and are therefore better equipped to make decisions about the individual's situation. It takes the power away from the person, and whose problem is it, anyway?

The giving of advice, sympathy and information leads to solutions without exploration. It is this **exploration** which is special and productive about counselling.

The more you understand people, the more you understand yourself.
The more you understand yourself, the more you understand people.

2

The manager as counsellor

Summary

The skills of people management and leadership revolve around the ability to make people successful and productive. Counselling belongs within this group of skills. In this chapter, we look at the qualities of a 'good' counsellor and compare them to the qualities of a 'good' manager. All the former apply to the latter, although there are additional skills that a manager does have to learn.

It is also important to look at the reasons why some managers choose to counsel, and what clie nts find attractive about counsellors. There are many managers who choose not to counsel. Whatever their reasons for making this choice, and it might be that this is a personal limitation, the importance of counselling as part of the manager's role should not be diminished. Discussing issues which will benefit the employee is not necessarily against the company interest. Although the organisation's purpose in life is not to satisfy its employees' needs, the well-being of its staff will be reflected in company productivity.

A 'good' counsellor:

- **understands why they are counselling**
- **knows their personal limitations**
- **knows their professional limitations**
- **has an understanding of why people come to them**
- **knows what skills and techniques they need to help people**
- **can progress understanding to action**
- **respects and accepts their 'clients'**
- **can negotiate appropriate boundaries of confidentiality.**

The role of the counsellor

A counsellor:

- **is aware of their own feelings**
- **is aware of their own intellectual abilities**
- **is imaginative in their approaches**
- **is comfortable and skilled when dealing with emotions – both their own and others**
- **respects their clients**
- **can integrate feeling, experience and behaviour**
- **is at home with people, in a one to one situation or in groups**
- **can progress understanding to action.**

The counsellor needs to understand their own reactions, before they can understand others. They need to be aware of their own abilities and parameters. They need to be open to change and new thought. They need to be able to turn theories into practical ideas that can help them to help others more effectively. They need to be able to help people put together their feelings, experiences and behaviour into an understandable framework. They need to be able to accept, and not judge. They need a wide range of interpersonal skills, but they also need the insight to know when to use them. They need to know when to listen and when to speak; when to invite and when to close down; when to watch and when to tell.

If this sounds like Superperson, it is. This is one version of an ideal. We do not live in an ideal world, and most people will fall short in one way or another at various different times. However, without an ideal, it is difficult to focus on a direction to be aimed for.

There is a fear that as counsellor, the manager will lose 'power'. Most of the time the manager is responsible for decision making, accepting responsibility for results, and using their charisma. As the manager, you possess the problem. The manager's role in counselling is to empower the client so that the client possesses the problem. This does not mean that the manager is powerless, it means that they have to take a different role. The actual shift for the manager is not in the qualities required, but in the role required.

What sort of issues bring out the role conflict for the manager as counsellor?

- decisiveness
- time pressures
- assessing line management issues
- 'extra work, few results'
- company culture
- personal style
- confidentiality.

Decisiveness

The company demands that the manager make and take decisions. It is impressed upon the manager that they must at all times be decisive.

On management training programmes it is possible to get managers to the stage where they are actually listening to what people are saying. However, as soon as you put them in any kind of work simulation, which demands a result, for most of them, the listening disappears and the task oriented manager reappears. It seems to be perceived that you cannot make decisions through listening!

Time pressures

20

The manager and the external counsellor may have different objectives. The manager may feel that an issue needs to be resolved instantly, and it doesn't matter whose intervention solves the problem. An external counsellor may feel they have the time to let the client sort things out for himself. Solving issues within a time limit, and using counselling techniques to solve a problem, are not mutually exclusive. Evaluating and improving performance does not mean telling clients how to do it. It means helping them find the best solution and commit themselves to it.

Assessing line management issues

A manager will often have to decide whether a client is bringing a request for the manager to act, or a request for help. (See the example below.)

Case study

Jeff was a project leader in a computer software company. He came to his manager and requested an extension on a project deadline. His manager had to assess whether Jeff:

- was giving him prior warning so that the manager could prepare himself, and reorganise connecting issues;
- could not organise or delegate tasks to his team properly, and so the work was not done;
- was not equipped to deal with the task, and was using the change of deadline to avoid facing this;
- was able to do the job. However, he was absorbed temporarily by personal issues, which were affecting his ability to do the job.

If the manager makes an assessment without finding out the facts, they potentially risk not only missing their deadline, but also the opportunity to help a subordinate function properly.

21

'Extra work, few results'

It is a lot easier for the manager to tell Jeff that he must pull himself together and meet the deadline, than to deal with a potential problem which the manager may not be able to deal with themselves. If there is a performance problem, the manager may first have to convince Jeff that he has a problem. It might just be yet another issue he has to deal with. All this might just make the manager feel that they would rather deal with it themselves.

Company culture

Sometimes the manager themselves may be a caring individual, but the company may have certain taboos about 'caring' behaviour. This might mean that even if the manager wanted to help, they would not be encouraged or supported by the company, and it might even damage their future prospects. This would only mean them setting themselves up for frustration.

Personal style

Sometimes this is not so much a conflict of role, as a personal conflict. For example, some managers do not feel that they have a genuine warmth for others. This might be due to shyness, inadequacy or an 'uncomfortable' feeling when discussing emotions.

Confidentiality

Confidentiality is an issue of prime importance to individuals. People often find it difficult to talk about themselves and are likely to find it even more difficult if they feel that the discussions will be disclosed.

So whose confidentiality is it? To whom does the interview material belong?

- To the counsellor/manager and individual alone?
- To the counsellor/manager and their manager?
- To the external counselling agency and the personnel department?

There is no easy answer to this question. Each case is different. What is consistent, however, is that a contract of confidentiality must be agreed between counsellor/manager and client, and the boundaries agreed and adhered to.

In courts, counsellors cannot claim privilege over matters disclosed to them by clients. It might be easier if there were such clear boundaries in the workplace! Where counsellors are working in settings where there are significant limitations on confidentiality, this fact must be shared with the individual from the beginning.

If, in the course of an interview, the client discloses information which might legally compromise the counsellor, then it is necessary for the counsellor to renegotiate the whole issue of confidentiality with the client. (See the example below.)

Case study

Joseph had been with his organisation for five years as a financial controller, with specific responsibility for petty cash and reimbursement expenditure. He asked to see his manager about what he described as 'a pressing matter'.

Joseph: I need to talk to you, but you must promise not to tell anyone.

The counsellor is now being asked to 'collude' with Joseph. It is very flattering to be told 'secrets', or be 'the only one who knows'. However, it is unlikely that the counsellor has the power to give Joseph the complete confidentiality he requests. Why is he requesting it? In a situation like this, there is only one response for the counsellor to make:

Counsellor: I cannot promise that, without knowing more about the situation. It may not be within my power to give you that promise.

By saying this, the counsellor has set a boundary, and the responsibility is back with the client. Joseph was trying to make a 'confession', which he would not have to do anything about. He would, however, feel better for telling someone, and the counsellor would be left holding the problem. Joseph was under severe financial and emotional pressure at home. He had been taking money from the petty cash and 'adjusting' the books. He was desperate to tell someone, but terrified he would lose his job. He therefore tried to use the confidentiality of the counselling inter-

23

view to protect himself. The counsellor made it clear at the beginning of the conversation that this was not an option, by refusing to give him carte blanche confidentiality. The discussion continued and, with the counsellor's perseverance, Joseph eventually 'confessed', and accepted that he was going to have to 'confess' officially and accept the consequences.

However, for most managers, the issue is not always as clear cut. The manager has potentially divided loyalties:

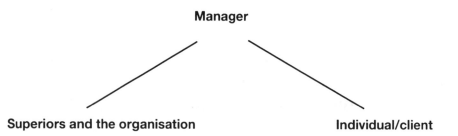

Employers have a legitimate interest in their employees' performance. If, therefore, an employee is not performing well and a manager counsels that employee to find out the reasons for this, why should the company not know of the consequences?

The answer to this incredibly complex problem, lies in the nature of what is reported back to the company. All the organisation needs to know, is how the employee is going to improve and what steps will be taken to ensure improvement. In this case, the company need only know the outcome of Stage Three of the interview. This is not as threatening to the client as the company knowing every intimate detail of the conversation.

There is no blanket answer to the question of divided loyalties, or role conflict. It constantly occurs when a manager is involved in internal counselling. Work pressures and conflicts of personality, and often fear and apprehension exist between manager and subordinate. It is not realistic to counsel someone in an atmosphere of fear and suspicion. This is a boundary for the manager's role as a counsellor.

Sometimes the manager sorts it out for themselves, while on other occasions, it may become too complex, and it might be appropriate for the manager to refer to an external counsellor.

It is not realistic to counsel someone in an atmosphere of fear and suspicion.

With all these complexities to juggle, what makes a manager want to counsel?

25

Why managers want to counsel

A need to 'do things to and for others'

Doctors and other professionals do things to or for their clients. This is not appropriate in the counselling role. It makes the counsellor the most powerful person, as they have the 'ability to do', and therefore prevents a reciprocal relationship. Some counsellors take on this excessive responsibility. Why?

Individuals who want to do something for the client are creating an inappropriate environment. Frequently, what they want to do for others, they would like to do themselves but, for various reasons, cannot or will not. They may counsel to fulfil needs of their own or fulfil some expectation of their own. This style will probably be ineffective because it is dealing with their own needs, and not the client's.

You cannot change other people's personalities. Neither can you change their experiences. You cannot even keep them from making mistakes or 'bad' decisions. You cannot provide happy endings. What you can provide is **an environment which allows people to take responsibility for their own lives without reproach**.

A desire to help people

There is no reason to deny the impulse to help others, or 'do good'. The ability to help someone come to a decision, or an acceptance, is a very strong motivator. It makes you feel good. What we are talking about is something that gives you satisfaction; like seeing a plant you have nurtured come to bloom. The difference is that you are using other people's lives to gain your satisfaction. This is OK, as long as your need to help does not outweigh the client's need. Your role is to facilitate, not to rescue or foster dependency.

You want people to like you

It is not unusual or unreasonable to look for a positive response from the individuals who come to see you. Difficult as it may be to admit, there are very few people who do not care what people think about them. This issue only becomes a problem if it overrides the client's need. It is necessary to create an environment which encourages people to talk. This can only happen when you are concerned enough about someone else to cease worrying about whether they like you or not.

One of the most important functions of the counsellor is to create a rapport between the client and themselves. Creating a rapport means supporting an environment that allows a free and honest exchange between counsellor and client. This does not mean that they have to 'be your friend', or indeed that they can be.

A need to judge others

Psychologist Elias Porter has suggested that our need to evaluate others is so much a part of ourselves, that we hardly know it is there. Because it is almost instinctive, this tendency can totally disrupt the non-judgmental nature of the counselling process. This need to evaluate is not the need to form an accurate diagnosis, but a deeper, less conscious need to compare yourself to others, and almost 'grade' your performance and other people's behaviour.

Passing judgement is about putting a value on persons or events. This value is based on *your* perceptions. This judgement is affected by your prejudices, experiences and unconscious motivations. You can see this almost reflex need to be critical in many everyday situations. For example, when you leave a seminar or meeting, the first question that comes to your lips may be, 'Well, what did you think of that? ...' The question is not a factual question such as 'What were they trying to put across?' but a more critical question.

27

In order to get the other person into focus, you have to **suspend judgement**. Too much evaluation also closes down the opportunity to learn about others and about life. If you feel you can put everything and everybody into boxes and categories, not only are you lulling yourself into a false sense of security, but you are limiting your effectiveness. Some of the signs of smugness and over-evaluation can be seen in remarks like:

"What a shame you did that ...'.

'Still, it's good that you can tell me these things ...'.

These are value judgements which do not progress the interview, and indeed may well disrupt it.

A need to give interpretations

This is really about a desire to let the client know (and also yourself) that you do understand what is going on. The unskilled counsellor will frequently use the same interpretation for various situations. For example, they may tell all their clients that they are going through a 'midlife crisis', and use this 'interpretation' to explain everything.

Skilled interpretation is a crucial part of the counselling process. The timing is extremely important. The risk of premature interpretation is that even though the interpretation may be right, it may be unacceptable because of bad timing. Most people resent having their behaviour interpreted, and can become defensive. Interpretations only work when clients are close to making and accepting those interpretations themselves.

So, while a motivator for counselling might be your need to display your interpretative skills to others, and make you feel powerful, it is unlikely to help the client and may cause them to withdraw.

A desire to find out about people

This might be subtitled 'human curiosity'. This refers to our curiosity about other people and how they operate. It can be very exciting to catch a glimpse of someone's private world, and can make you feel very powerful. This is sometimes signalled by over-excessive questioning without space for the client to be heard. Obviously counselling cannot proceed without any questions. It is the way they are asked, and how appropriate they are, that is the key to the counsellor's motivation in asking them.

A need to reassure people

This is one of the most powerful motives for counselling. It is very comforting to feel that you are in a position to 'make people feel better'. One of the most important functions of the counselling process is to be supportive. Being supportive is a very active process. It is not about reassuring noises like 'there, there' or 'don't worry, it will be all right'. This is non-supportive reassurance, and only tells people that they need not feel the way they are feeling. In doing this, it denies their feelings, and devalues their experience. This is *not* constructive support, because if you deny the problem, then you cannot help the client deal with it!

In a more complex vein, some counsellors use the process to reassure themselves, by reassuring others. This goes on at an unconscious level, and occurs when a counsellor has issues of their own they need to resolve. Instead of dealing with the issues themselves, they deal with other people's problems. This sometimes makes them feel that their problems are not so great, or by reassuring others, they are reassuring themselves. This is an important dynamic for the counsellor to be aware of, as it will prevent any work being done with the client.

Real support comes from listening to people as they explore their thoughts, and not backing away when the experience looks like being difficult for you. Giving false or empty reassurance does not help the client or yourself; in fact it increases the counsellor's stress.

Every counsellor, no matter how learned or experienced, has a limit, a personal parameter. This is not about professional boundaries, but more

Real support comes from listening to people as they explore their thoughts.

about recognition of the fact that there is a limit to what you can do. There will be some people you will not be able to help, even with referral. No one is expected to succeed all the time. Because you are dealing with human beings, 'success' is far less tangible than how many units you can sell. Personal growth, by its very nature, is limited, and never takes place overnight.

The more you know about yourself, the more appropriate will be your expectations of your performance. People sometimes feel guilty when they fall short of their ideal. But is their ideal unrealistic? It is important to review realistically the limits of your abilities. What can you actually do for people?

- Can you take away their many experiences?
- Can you change their backgrounds or take away real grief?
- Can you compensate them for bad luck?
- Can anyone remove the obstacles that are found in everyone's life?

You cannot have an answer about your own capacity to help others, unless you are realistic about the things you cannot change. There are some people you can't help, some people who you will never be able to establish a relationship with. This is a commonsense approach to people and your own limitations.

What makes people want to be counselled by a particular counsellor?

There are many things that 'attract' clients to counsellors. You may appear attractive because of physical characteristics and appearance; for example, you are good looking and well groomed. You may be attractive due to your position, qualifications or title; for example, personnel manager, psychologist. Sometimes the attraction is due to a similar experience, or career pattern. Sometimes you are spontaneously attracted to someone because of a 'bundle' of things, such as age, friendliness, accepting behaviour, admiration. When asked to identify the reasons you might say, 'I don't know why, I just like her ...'

These types of attraction, as with the attractions of similar age and interests, can be both positive, and alienating. They are only helpful to the relationship if they are supported by respect and trust.

People may be drawn to you because of your reputation for insight and understanding; i.e. through previous clients' reports. It is this reputation for being 'trustworthy' that is the most important, and hardest to define. Like other counselling skills, being perceived as trustworthy is a crucial management skill. It is this trust that inspires people to work for their bosses, and is a dilute form of charismatic power.

Being able to trust your counsellor means:

- **Confidentiality:** The client can say, 'Whatever I say to this person about myself, they will not tell anyone else without my permission.'
- **Use of power:** The client can feel, 'If I trust this person with myself, they will not abuse that information, and will use it in my interest.'
- **Credibility:** The client can say, 'I can believe what he says.'
- **Understanding**: The client can feel, 'This person is listening to me, and is trying to understand me.'

The terms for being perceived as 'untrustworthy' are the reverse of these. For example, 'I can't trust them, they always look so untidy and disorganised.' Or, ' You can't trust her, she'll tell your boss everything.'

How do you establish trust?

- Make a contract with the client and stick to it.
- Be realistic about the client's, and your own, abilities.
- Provide clients with the kind of structure that makes them feel safe, and thereby allows them to contribute to the 'helping' process. This is part of 'empowerment'. It makes the client feel a part of a process, rather than someone who is being 'worked on'. One way of providing a structure is a clear client counsellor contract. This way both parties know exactly what to expect from the process. (For details of contract setting, see Chapter 4.)
- Behave in a way which the client can emulate: for example, listening to clients, accepting what they say, communicating understanding. This leads to respect and trust.
- Maintain confidentiality.
- Never promise anything you cannot deliver.

A trusting relationship allows the client to speak more, and feel at ease with the counsellor. The process is circular; encourage the client to speak and show you are listening, and they will speak more. This is because they trust, and are drawn to, the counsellor.

Generally, clients believe that the counsellor has some information, knowledge, or skill to help them. Sometimes this 'reputation' comes from their role or title, for example, psychotherapist, counsellor. Sometimes the 'reputation' comes from word of mouth, or by association. Neither a role nor a perceived reputation are guarantees of competence.

Sometimes clients experience the way a counsellor behaves as competency; for example, the language the counsellor uses, or the counsellor's own confidence. These indicators may well be true, but the only evidence for it lies in the actual achievements of the counsellor. They have to be able to deliver whatever they set out to do in the contract. This is where the counsellor's own motivation for wanting to counsel comes into play.

The attraction works both ways, and if a counsellor perceives himself to be attractive to one client, but not to another, he may tend to be less demanding of attractive clients and less likely to listen to unattractive clients. The sense of attraction, whether to or from the client, can distract the counsellor from the needs of the client. It might make the counsellor 'perform' rather than listen, or say things he thinks the client wants to hear, rather than what is appropriate

Sometimes individuals will bring problems that are similar to those of the counsellor/manager. This might affect the manager in many ways: they may try and solve their own problem through the client, or hear their perceptions of their own situation, rather than those of the individual. Either way, if a similarity of problem gets in the way of the manager's ability to help, they should refer the person to someone else.

... the individual human being is of value ... it is important that each individual should be able to develop his own personality in as unrestricted and complete a way as possible.

ANTHONY STORR

3

Where can counselling help?

Summary

Situations occur at work, triggered off by events both at work and outside of work, that result in differences in an individual's behaviour. When this results in a loss of productivity and /or well-being of an individual or group, it is the manager's role to assess the situation and deal with it appropriately.

In this chapter, we look at some of the situations that may give rise to counselling. A 'good' manager will be able to recognise patterns of behaviour which might be dealt with by counselling. Although it is not possible to predict people's behaviour with certainty, there are some situations which will cause problems for most people, most times they occur. It is also true that certain issues, such as changes in the work environment or personal life, will have an effect on people's work performance.

The three main types of situation that arise are:

- issues from the organisation
- issues from the individual's own personality
- issues from the individual's external environment.

Where counselling can help

Case study

Sarah Longstone was brought in to take charge of the computer department in a medium sized engineering firm. In her late twenties, Sarah had considerable experience working in a range of mainframe computer systems, whilst her hobby as a voluntary supervisor in a sports centre had given her some experience of management. But this was her first post as a manager and the first woman the firm had appointed to such a level.

Although very confident in her new job, Sarah encountered some problems. Her immediate boss understood the department's work but was extremely busy and often away on business trips. The director to whom he reported and to whom Sarah reported in his absence knew little of computer technology; his authoritarian and dismissive attitude towards some of the department staff created a good deal of open resentment towards him.

The computer system used in the department was in some respects new to Sarah, but particularly with her boss away so much, she was for many months too busy to settle down and learn it as thoroughly as she might have wished. She still felt she was having to catch up. Then, although most of the department staff were friendly from the beginning, two experienced male colleagues made it plain that they had each wanted her job. They lost no time in telling her that she was inadequately qualified. One in particular continued to imply that a woman should not be in the post and that she should get herself a decent boyfriend and stay at home.

Some of these problems eased with time and the work continued to be very interesting. She gained people's respect and trust and the firm relied on her. But some things did not change; the workload remained heavy and the long hours greatly curtailed her leisure time. She had a boyfriend and he pointed out that they now had much less time together and she seemed to put her job before him. She remained very isolated at work. After two years she concluded that she would not be able to change these adverse features and also that she would be unlikely to be promoted further. With nobody in the firm to talk to, she was beginning to listen to the headhunters who phoned her from time to time pointing out where else she could be employed ...

Case study

James Prushaw was a competent fifty-three year old office manager. He worked as second-in-command in a country office of what was until recently a successful medium sized distribution company. James had kept up with modern technology and was very adept at using information technology. He was respected and trusted by his older staff, his clients and in his local community. His three children had all left home and were working in London.

Last year, James's firm was taken over by a much larger company seeking to extend its coverage of provincial areas. He tried to view this development positively and to welcome the wider experience and new ideas it might bring. But actually what he experienced was a growing number of rules and constraints on how he was required to operate. There was also increasing pressure to develop more business at the cost, it seemed to him, of customer service. However, he continued to work hard, indeed to work longer and longer hours, and looked forward to taking over the office when his boss retired. Then two things happened. The board of the major company in which he was now employed, decided on a policy of office rationalisation and the development of a more dynamic, youthful image. James's office was given notice of closure and the staff were told they would be transferred to another of the company's offices at the other end of town.

James's boss decided to take early retirement but James was not promoted. Instead, a younger member of staff took over and James was offered a job which was, effectively, a demotion.

Meanwhile, there were issues for him at home. Before her children were born, James's wife was a floor manager in a large department store. She loved her work and always said she would try to go back to it once the children were launched. Once they had left home she began to look around. She then accepted an interesting job in her brother's shop some 200 miles away, and proposed to stay with him during the week and 'see how it goes'. She pointed out that, especially with James working longer and longer hours, home for her was just a lonely round of boring domestic chores. She said it was high time she started living for herself again.

James felt unable to cope with these experiences and became increasingly withdrawn and unresponsive, both at work and at home.

Sarah and James are both valuable employees and their employers, at least, know how valuable they are. But they are now subject to considerable strains due to the cumulative effect of major social and technological developments operating in combination with doubtless sound management decisions.

The result is that one of them is gradually becoming less effective whilst Sarah is deciding to leave. Their stories are not unusual and many of their colleagues will have undergone similar experiences and share something of their feelings.

Enlightened self-interest should be enough to interest employers of such staff in ways of relieving the strains they experience. Among the measures they could consider, counselling must surely come high on the list. Whether or not the wider circumstances can be changed, counselling can help individuals to make constructive moves to ease their own situation, or at least to accept what must be accepted. It can speed the process of coming to terms with change and check the development of damaging reactions which rebound upon other staff. In these terms, counselling is not a luxury service, nor even a humane element in a good personnel programme, but simply sound business practice.

Why individuals may need counselling

The circumstances which affect employees are by now well known. Our population structure has changed and jobs have changed. Technology has altered the skills we need and the conditions under which we work. New attitudes to careers and family life are affecting everyone in employment. The word 'job' may even disappear. Many organisations are moving away from structures made up of jobs to areas of work that need to be done. In the fast white-water of today's and tomorrow's economy, jobs can become a rigid solution to an elastic problem.

But, in general, the challenge of adapting to these changes has been considered in terms of policies and practices, rather than the impact on individuals. We have some idea of what we should be doing about recruitment (i.e. the opposite of what many companies are now doing, which is to engage in an increasingly expensive scramble after graduates) and about training and retraining and the analysis of job skills and competencies. Companies have accepted some responsibility for easing the pains of redundancy and relocation. But we have paid less attention to the strains which demographic and technological changes are imposing on those remaining in employment, who are expected to see the organisation through the white rapids into calmer water.

> *A great deal of time is spent on strategic decision making, but disproportionately little time on the people who will have to implement such decisions..*

The change from functional management to process management, along with a loss of both hierarchies and clear career structures, creates new and less tangible problems for the manager. These are above and beyond their responsibility for the business 'bottom line'. A great deal of time is spent on strategic decision making, but disproportionately little time on the people who will have to implement such decisions.

There is also a tendency to concentrate on people's technical skills, as opposed to interpersonal skills. Of course technical skill is essential, but **people do not work in a vacuum**. There are other people around, both in the workplace and in their private lives, and they affect the way people work.

An effective and stimulating manager learns through experience, and is able to recognise patterns of events and situations which could lead to problems. With individuals, however, this is somewhat more difficult, because no two individuals are the same. It is therefore difficult to 'predict' behaviour with the same certainty as you might predict computer problems.

There are numerous theories on behaviour prediction, ranging from Freud to John Hunt (for further information on these areas, see Appendix V). Freud, for example, felt that there were two important factors in the formation of groups and organisations:

- **Issues with leadership:** The group cannot form unless a leader has been established and accepted.
- **Issues with relationships:** Once everyone accepts the leader, they then have to agree their common focus and their working relationships.

Professor Hunt felt that various circumstances and values created people's motivation to work. If these circumstances or values changed, or were forced to change, then it would have an effect on the individual's behaviour. For example, if it was important for someone to work as part of a team, and they were suddenly told that they would now be working on their own, this would probably have a marked effect on their work.

There seem to be three separate people issues:

---

1 **Issues coming from the organisation e.g. restructuring, promotion, demotion, policy changes.**
2 **Issues coming from the individual's own personality e.g. individual behaviour patterns.**
3 **Issues coming from the individual's external environment e.g. moving, marriage, loss.**

These issues, in turn, seem to consist of three common elements:

- a difficult situation
- a fundamentally 'normal' person
- the failure of the normal psychological mechanisms the individual normally uses to handle such situations.

41

In other words, there are some situations which would upset most people. It is the manager/counsellor's role to distinguish between transient problems and those of a more disabling nature. For example, is the problem the individual is experiencing, one which is situational and which they will be able to deal with in the course of time? Or is it more serious, in that the individual is stuck and cannot understand why the situation is so difficult for them? People experiencing a 'situational disturbance' cannot quite tell what is wrong, although they do recognise behaviours that are not characteristic of them. The counsellor has to be careful not to give mere reassurance, as this might undermine the person. They also have to be wary of over-diagnosis of a situation which is not as bad as the counsellor is making out. Once again the counsellor is obliged to listen. Listen to the context in which the incident(s) occurs. Is this isolated? Has it happened before? Have they dealt with it before? Are the circumstances different? etc.

One of the mysteries of life is the fact that people carry on, despite enormous emotional and psychological burdens. Some individuals can handle severe blows to their self-esteem, and still come back with confidence. Others find everything a struggle and the slightest thing can throw them off beam, so that they cannot continue with everyday activities.

Past experiences are also a good guide to people's reactions. Those who have suffered 'the slings and arrows of outrageous fortune', and have learned the hard way about the way life can give or take away things that are sought after, are generally better equipped to deal with change. Ordinary stresses of life are easier to cope with if there are some options or available solutions. Most people cope better with choices. It is when the choices are removed, that stress has its greatest effect.

When someone is going through some situational problem, the chief reaction is anxiety, although it takes many forms. These range from restlessness, irritability, an inability to concentrate, to a preoccupation with detail. They sometimes go through physiological symptoms of anxiety; for example, loss of sleep, tiredness, under-eating, overeating.

Sometimes people are surprised by new events or behaviours in their lives and they resort to activities which compound their problems. For example, someone who gets into fights at work in order to deal with problems at home. Despite the fact that a person's behaviour might stem from any one or more of these categories, the presenting behaviours are likely to be the same. For example, if someone is very preoccupied with moving home, their disinterested behaviour at work might be similar to someone who is having difficulty dealing with their workload, because it is beyond their capability.

What situations then, might prompt a need to counsel staff? Typical situations include the following:

- people not performing to their usual standard
- persistent lateness
- inability to communicate clearly
- inability to act as part of a team
- unusual or changed behaviour
- inability to take or make decisions
- change in personal circumstances
- change in work circumstances.

Such situations are likely to involve the following issues:

- marital problems
- bereavement
- drinking
- drugs
- health
- emotional adjustment
- inability to cope
- lack of skill/ability
- career crisis
- lack of direction.

The following kinds of behaviours should signal to you a need for counselling:

- The individual is eager to please, wants to help rather than do, looking for a friend, cannot accept success, constantly worries about failure, dependent on others, indecisive, avoids responsibility, always taking on new work, never completes to deadlines, constantly at meetings.
- The individual is aggressive, talks at you, does not listen, bosses others, obstinate, fixed views and opinions, auto-

cratic, unwilling to delegate, critical and contemptuous of others, unreasoned, envious, cannot take criticism.

- The individual cannot organise own work properly, blames others constantly, finds it difficult to finish jobs, defensive, secretive, has few friends, irrational, prone to panic, avoids personal contact, unco-operative, sometimes deprecating about the organisation, uses memos, puts off work, anxious.

All of these are behaviours, or symptoms, of an issue that has to be dealt with. It is not an exhaustive list, but raises some of the potential times when counselling may be appropriate. However, it is not just the issues which determine whether counselling is the appropriate path to take, we need to look at the circumstances and the manager's own position when deciding how to deal with the situation.

4

Setting a framework

Summary

Setting boundaries at the beginning of any relationship is crucial to achieving results. It establishes direction and allows all those involved to measure achievement. It makes explicit the ground rules for the relationship and avoids misunderstanding and false expectations. This becomes even more important in the counsellor/manager role, as there is so much room for misinterpretation.

45

In order to set a framework, you must:

- state the parameters of the relationship at the beginning of the relationship
- describe the proposed outcomes, norms and procedures
- state explicitly the confidentiality and the roles of the counsellor and client
- ensure the environment encourages freedom to speak.

Setting the boundaries

Starting a counselling relationship is like starting any relationship, whether it is professional or personal. For both people to get the best from the relationship, they need to set guidelines, or boundaries, which describe the type of relationship that each person wants. If these guidelines are not set or discussed, inevitable misunderstandings occur. Setting the boundaries for the time spent together is the most crucial point of the relationship, and covers the following areas:

- what will and won't be covered during the time
- what the manager and 'client' should expect as outcomes
- length of time to be spent together
- procedures
- what behaviours are acceptable
- levels of confidentiality
- frequency of meeting
- responsibility.

46

> **Without this framework, there is no way of measuring what has been achieved, or indeed focusing on the issues.**

People do not feel secure without boundaries, and will not deem it 'safe' to talk unless they are sure how far they can go, or in what direction they are travelling. This boundary setting is sometimes called contracting, as an agreement or contract has to be agreed by both parties about what they expect and need from each other. Without this 'contract', you risk raised expectations, false hopes and miscommunication.

> **The rest of the relationship will not flow, proceed or be measurable in terms of results unless an initial contract is set.**

Sometimes people avoid making a contract as they feel it might inhibit the process, or make the format too rigid. The reverse is true. Too fluid, or lack of, a contract makes it difficult to progress. If the terms of the contract change, then renegotiate. For example, if you begin by saying that everything is completely confidential, and then the individual brings up an issue which may require you to involve someone else, then you have to renegotiate the contract terms to accommodate a change in circumstances. If you do not, the relationship will be broken, because you will have broken the contract.

47

Types of boundary

Having established the importance of boundaries, it is necessary to decide on the main boundaries that need to be established at the start of any meeting together. These will generally include the following:

- **outcomes**
- **confidentiality**
- **role of the counsellor**
- **norms of the meeting**
- **procedure of the meeting**

Outcomes

This involves discussion from both parties about what they are expecting as a result of the meeting. It will be largely initiated by the interviewer, but must be agreed by the client, in order to avoid misunderstanding. It is at this stage that you should discuss what each person expects from the session. It is important to identify the possible and eliminate the impossible, for example, making it clear that the session is not about cementing friendships. For example:

> *'At the end of the session, the counsellor and client will have agreed on the appropriate direction for the client's career to take.'*

> *'During the hour we have booked to talk to one another, we will have a chance to analyse the issues that are holding me back, and look at ways of dealing with them.'*

Confidentiality

This is a statement about who, if anyone, will hear any outcomes or information from the session. **It must be stated at the outset of the meeting**. If there is any change to the status of the parameters of confidentiality, then the boundaries have to be renegotiated.

For example, if a client made allegations of sexual harassment about a member of staff, in order to investigate them fully it would probably be necessary to involve other people, as well as the counsellor. This means that the counsellor and the client would have to agree on who else might be privy to the information. If the client did not agree to this and the counsellor felt that it would not be possible to proceed without input from other people, then they would have to discuss again whether an outcome would be possible without renegotiating the terms of confidentiality.

Role of the counsellor

This is an explanation of the role that the counsellor will take on during the session. This establishes two points:

1 The role of the counsellor as an individual: If, for example, you are the client's line manager, it is very important to describe any differences between the two roles.

2 The part that the counsellor will take in the discussion: This means indicating to the client that the responsibility for any outcomes of the interview will rest with the client, and describing the 'non-directive approach' (see Chapter 3).

49

Norms of the meeting

This involves describing what sorts of behaviours are acceptable in the session, if they differ from the norm that the client might expect. If, for example, swearing, smoking and emotional outbursts are not normally acceptable, but you feel that those behaviours might be appropriate in the counselling interview, you must state it. Like all items in the contract, boundaries should be *explicit*, not implicit.

Structures of the session

The counsellor should explain the structure of the interview; what sort of stages the session will have and what will happen at those stages in the session. For example, they might describe the session in terms of the three stage process:

1 That it will begin by discussing and exploring the client's situation, in order to identify the issues that have to be dealt with.

2 They will then spend time focusing on the issues, trying to understand and clarify them.

Only after having done this, will the session be able to move to the third stage, which involves:

3 Discussing the options open to the client, to deal with the situation (for more detail, see Chapter 7).

They should also explain what will happen at the end of the session.

Time

The individual should be told how much time they have at that particular session. They should also be told whether any further time is available, and if so, under what circumstances. It is also helpful to say what time you will finish. It is not possible to legislate on how long a counselling session 'should' take. Most professional counselling sessions last an hour. Sessions that go on longer than this, tend to be less and less productive as time goes on. There will be times when you do not need to spend an hour with a client. Gauging time in an interview is very difficult, and it is important to be flexible. While this time does not have to be adhered to rigidly, it is worth remembering as a benchmark.

Once established, the purpose of boundaries is to stick to them. If something is contracted, you must **keep to it and be seen to keep to it**. For example, if you agree to spend an hour, spend it. Like children, adults will test boundaries to see if they really are safe. The only way to change them is to renegotiate the terms of the contract.

The contract has to be stated and *explicit*, not implicit.

It may be necessary to restate some of the contract terms at the beginning of any subsequent sessions. During a session, if the discussions stray from their purpose, not only is it useful to have the contract to bring you back to base, it is also a way of ensuring that you don't become involved in inappropriate areas.

Environment for the interview

Part of the boundary setting is setting the environment for the interview. The two most important factors for this are privacy, and security and comfort.

Privacy

The most important environmental element is privacy. 'Counselling', in a diluted form, often takes place in corridors, but any serious work has to be done in privacy.

Privacy does not only mean a room with just you and the individual in it. Privacy means:

- **confidentiality**
- **no interruptions or distractions**
- **time.**

Confidentiality

If this word keeps occurring in this book, it is with good reason. One of people's greatest fears when they go to talk to someone about an issue, is that 'everyone' will know about it. If they wanted everyone to know about it, they would have told everyone. It is also important to strike a balance between stating and overstating confidentiality to the point where the individual feels 'Why do they keep stating this? Is there some doubt here?'

The best proof of confidentiality is in the reality. Does anyone, other than those people agreed by counsellor and client, get to hear of what happened in the interview? If not, then you have the glimmerings of a trusting relationship. However, all too often, particularly in large organisations, people are highly suspicious of what, in the past, may have been empty pronouncements of confidentiality. For this reason they have developed (sometimes rightly) a cynical view of statements of confidentiality. This makes it hard for the interviewer to gain trust. It is essential that the counsellor never promises things they cannot deliver, or promises confidentiality that is inappropriate or not possible. The counsellor does not lose trust by being honest, rather they gain respect.

> **The only way to establish confidentiality is to be seen to be keeping your word.**

This takes time and perseverance, and the old adage that trust is earned, not given, is very important to remember.

No interruptions or distractions

People need to feel that they are being heard and listened to. This means that the counsellor has to keep his mind on the client and not on himself. In order to do this, you need not only to create an inviting and welcoming environment for the client, but also to create an environment for yourself whereby you can take the time to deal wholeheartedly with the person in front of you.

This means ensuring that:

- the phone does not ring during the interview
- you do not look about the room or out of the window
- no one interrupts
- you do not keep looking at your watch
- you do not shuffle papers or notes
- you concentrate on the client.

Time

This means quality of time, not just the fact that you are spend-ing, for example, 30 minutes with this person (which to some people is almost enough in itself), but also that this 30 minutes will be devoted to this person.

53

It means seeing them on time and not keeping them waiting. This not only makes people feel devalued, but also makes them tense.

It means ensuring you have enough time to see them, and that after seeing them you have a few minutes to collect your thoughts before your next appointment, so that you don't spend the last ten minutes of the session thinking about your next appointment.

This becomes very important in the light of something we call 'the hand on the door syndrome'. This describes the event when the individual talks and maybe even rambles at great length during their allotted time, but just as they are about to leave the session, with their hand on the door, they tell you what is really worrying them. By doing this, they have given you their prob-lem without having to do anything about it themselves.

By telling you about the problem, they feel better temporarily as they feel they have offloaded it. However, by doing this they are not dealing with the problem at all, and their relief will only be temporary. If you listen carefully during the last ten minutes of a session, you may sometimes recognise the signs of a potential 'offloading'; phrases like 'by the way', 'actually', 'well it doesn't really matter because ...'. This syndrome does not by any means occur every time, or even regularly, but it is very important to be aware of it. So why do they do it?

Often it is a means of testing out how the counsellor will react, and to see whether the counsellor has been listening to them. But the major reason is to try to 'dump' the problem somewhere, without having to deal with it. How do you deal with it?

54

There is only one way to deal with it, and that is to tell the client what they have done: you have to ask them why they have waited until that time to make such an important point. This, however, is not appropriate if you do not have the time to deal with it there and then. If you do not have the time, then it is best to acknowledge their comments, and say that you will look at them next time you speak together. (And make sure you do!) Whichever option you take, you must acknowledge the comments.

This gives rise to a very important issue in counselling, which is covered in more detail in Chapter 5, and that is the issue of the **presenting problem**.

When you initially negotiate a contract, it will probably be based on what is called the 'presenting problem'. This means the problem that has either been identified by you, the client, or their boss as something that has to be sorted out. This could be anything from a slackening of performance to an inability to communicate with colleagues. This is known as 'the presenting problem'.

Almost invariably this is not the real underlying problem, but until you have mutually agreed what that is, you will negotiate the initial contract based on the presenting problem. Because the goal posts are likely to change, it is as well to be aware of this at the outset, and be prepared for renegotiation. For example, you may have organised a counselling session with someone who said they wanted to discuss their promotion prospects. When you begin talking, however, it transpires that they are feeling terribly under pressure and can't cope with their workload. This means you will have to agree this with the client, and agree what you feel can be discussed at that session, and redefine possible outcomes.

Security and comfort

The session has to be seen as taking place in a slightly different atmosphere from discussions about work schedules and costings. For these discussions, it may be your custom to sit behind your desk. This is not the most appropriate way of counselling. Why? Because it can imbue the interviewer with an authority which does not encourage a completely honest atmosphere.

While they see you as the authority figure, it is difficult for a client to see how something they say in this environment will not be 'held against them', because of the power of the authority. So not only does it place a physical barrier between you and the individual, and potentially a psychological one, it also does not encourage an atmosphere whereby the

It may be your custom to sit behind your desk. This is not the most appropriate way of counselling.

person feels that anything they say will be accepted. This is especially true with managers who are used to using their authority to get results. All too often, managers keep behind the desk because they themselves feel 'safer' there.

It is more appropriate to sit in chairs at an angle to the client, so that you are not facing them 'head-on' in an aggressive way.

A great deal has been written about setting up environments and body language (see Chapter 5). Whilst it is important not to overreact, it is equally important not to dismiss it. If you consider personal experiences, you will remember times when you have felt that someone's presence was 'threatening', or that you felt 'comfortable' with a particular situation. These responses are to do with feeling 'in control' of the situation. Your role as a counsellor is to help the client feel 'in control' of their situation so that they can deal with it. Creating an environment where they feel relaxed is crucial. A simple action like sitting too close, or too far away, could destroy that environment.

So we have established the need for a statement of purpose and procedure at the beginning of the session. How do you do it?

> **All you have to do is state and agree the terms of the contract with the client at the beginning of the meeting.**

This means stating the terms and checking these are acceptable to the client. They should be stated baldly, with no frills or apologies, just as they are. This is important, as it is crucial to avoid misunderstandings. Therefore the language should be simple and the sentences short. (Those rules might easily apply to the whole process of counselling.)

An example of a possible contract is shown opposite:

This example covers some of the areas we have been talking about, and puts them into practical terms.

So far we have only looked at contracting in terms of the beginning of the meeting. However, ending the session is as important as the beginning. While this is covered in detail in Chapter 7, it is important to remember that you may need to restate some of the initial contract. This is not only as a summary device, to show the individual what has happened, it is also a way of proving the necessity of the initial contract, and may also be a time to renegotiate. Without the initial contract as a bench-mark, it is impossible to see how far you have come, or how far you have strayed from the initial objectives of the interview.

Timing	One hour
Frequency	Once a fortnight; initially for four sessions
Purpose	To review progress on time management
Method	Discussion and analysis of critical incidents
Venue	Manager's office
Role of counsellor	Facilitator – not line manager
Role of client	Ownership of responsibility

All matters discussed to remain between counsellor and client only.

No note taking during interview, unless by agreement.

After each session, a summary of agreed points to be written up by counsellor and held by client.

Imagine yourself alone in the midst of nothingness, and then tell me how large you are.

A. S. Eddington

5

Understanding the situation

Summary

Once a manager has established a need for counselling, and set the boundaries, they need to consider how to actually go about it. In this chapter, we look at Stage One and Stage Two of a counselling session. These are about getting the story from the client and then establishing and focusing on the real situation.

Until the 'real situation' is identified and agreed, you don't know what you are dealing with, and therefore how to deal with it. Getting the story involves listening to and observing the client. It means hearing what the person is really saying and not what you want them to say. It means getting an accurate drawing of the client and reflecting it back to them. You need to be able to help the individual focus on the issues and enable them to identify and understand what the situation is really about. This chapter establishes the techniques and skills necessary to enable both manager and 'client' to deal with the issue.

The main skills for the counsellor to use are:

- **active listening**
- **observing**
- **specific, appropriate questioning**
- **reactive and empathic responding**

Introduction

It is important to remember that the counsellor should avoid applying theories in a textbook way. This makes the counsellor anxious to do well, and in doing so, they lose sight of their main purpose, which is the client's needs. The counsellor's biggest strength is their own personality. So look at some of the guidelines and use your intuition within their framework. Make the guidelines your own. How do you start?

First of all, it would probably be helpful to break down the elements of the session into three stages. Although we are calling this the 'counselling session', it applies to any discussions, whether formal or informal.

There are three stages to the counselling process:

1 **Getting the story:** listening, interpreting, responding.
2 **Understanding the situation:** exploring, focusing, giving feedback.
3 **Moving on:** developing strategies, gaining acceptance.

This chapter deals with the first two stages of the process and the third stage of the process is dealt with in Chapter 7.

Stage One – Getting the story

The manager aims to establish a rapport with the individual by giving them attention, listening, and responding. Because of the way the manager responds, the client is encouraged to explore specifically their thoughts, behaviour and experiences, which relate to the current situation.

In order to get the story, the manager needs the skills of:

> - **'active' listening**
> - **open questioning**
> - **observing**
> - **non-judgmental responding**
> - **reflecting**
> - **paraphrasing**
> - **summarising.**

61

The client has come to you and at this stage is unlikely to be clear about what their problem is, or how to deal with it. It is very much the counsellor's role at this point to help the client tell their story.

This means overriding your instinctive 'automatic sorting system'. Normally, you have picked up a great deal of information about people and events and you use this information to enable you to respond quickly to situations. In the counselling interview, you need to suspend this instinctive behaviour, to enable you to hear how *the client* perceives the situation. It is *their* perceptions at this stage that are important.

Take, for example, the presenting problem of Howard.

Case study

Howard has always been a totally devoted worker. His work performance has slumped dramatically recently. Is it because he is trying to do
too much? Is he capable of completing his workload? Is his job too big?
Is he going through any changes outside of work that might affect his
performance? How do you know which is the cause and will your treatment be different?

Finding out what the problem is, is the first part of a counselling session. Of course you could make assumptions, based

on your past knowledge of Howard, but they might be wrong
and you could end up dealing with the wrong problem. The
point to remember is that, although the presenting behaviours
are similar, the causes may be very different and may require
different approaches to deal with them.

Bearing in mind that this stage is about finding out what the
client is there for, the most important skills required are **Listening** and **hearing**.

Active listening

This could be a definition for counselling or management itself.
It is at the heart of the counselling process and, without it, it is
unlikely that any situation will be sorted out.

> **'Active' listening is a set of techniques through which
> one person can obtain information from another. They
> can be used by the listener to control the direction and
> flow of the conversation and the amount and depth of
> information disclosed.**

Listening is perceived by many to be a 'passive' skill: i.e. you are supposed to sit and absorb the information being transmitted, without any input. This is *not* the case. The objective of the listener is to:

- **give the speaker every opportunity to speak**
- **demonstrate interest in what is being said**
- **avoid intruding their own information, interpretations or concerns directly.**

Give the speaker every opportunity to speak

Human beings have a kind of 'hierarchy of communications'. This means that in establishing relationships, you have to go through stages in order to develop the relationship further. It is represented as a pyramid.

63

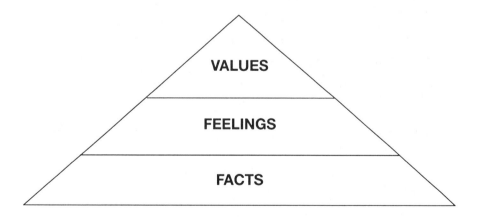

Facts

Most of your relationships in life will not develop past this stage. This is the stage where you only exchange factual information about yourself for factual information about others. For example, the first question we inevitably ask people when we meet them for the first time, is 'What do you do?'. The reason why we need to begin with facts, is that they are tangible realities and are therefore unlikely to be threatening in any way. In some way they seem to be 'external' and 'visible'.

Feelings

This is the stage in communication when you can begin to ask questions that relate to how people feel. For example, 'How did you feel when that happened?'. People find it too threatening to be asked 'feelings' questions, without first having gone through the 'facts' stage.

Values

This is a stage in the communication process which you will share with a very small number of people. This level of communication concerns your motivation for doing things, the kinds of issues that are important to you, and why they are important. It is this level of communication that provides the counsellor with the 'essence' of the client. You *cannot* bypass the facts and feelings stages and go straight to this stage. Why?

- they wouldn't tell you
- it wouldn't make any sense if they did!

If a person says to you out of the blue, 'I've always found it important to tell the truth at all times ...', you do not know a great deal more about the person, except the 'value judgement'. You also do not know:

- whether this is true, as you have no evidence
- why it is important
- the implications that this has for them in their working life.

That is why it becomes important to use the 'funnelling' technique.

If you turn the pyramid upside down, then you have a structure for obtaining information in a discussion. This is called a funnel, because you are narrowing down the information until you get the distilled bit at the end of the funnel. In reality, any interaction or interview is likely to contain many 'funnels', as you look for different pieces of information to build up a picture of the person you are talking to.

This funnelling can be best achieved according to the type of questions asked. The most appropriate type of question for this stage is the open-ended question. This is dutifully referred to by most managers as a question which cannot be answered with a simple 'yes' or 'no'. This is true, but it is also much more than that. It is, as its name suggests, a way of opening up a particular subject area.

65

These questions normally begin with the words, *how, what, why, when, where, who*. For example:

- 'What sort of projects have you been working on this month?'
- 'How did that affect your relationship with other members of the team?'

One important aspect of these questions is that they are all specific i.e. they relate to a particular event or task. This is very important. If a question is put in a vague way, you will get a vague answer. This is because it is very difficult to answer vague questions any other way! It is also a reason for avoiding excessive use of 'why' questions. Not only can they sound accusatory, for example: 'Why did you do it that way?' but also, they are hard to answer because they are abstract. For example, it is quite difficult to answer the question, 'Why do you like your job?', because it is an abstract concept. If you rephrase it to 'What is it you like about your job?', it becomes more specific and concrete and therefore easier to answer.

THE FUNNEL

START WITH A GENERAL EASY OPEN-ENDED QUESTION

'Tell me about ...'
'What sort of tasks did that involve?'
Check key responsibilities, purpose and outcome

LISTEN
and observe
FOLLOW UP
LISTEN
Listen for emotive or key words

CHECK FACTUAL DETAILS

Ask about what they actually did

'What were your personal tasks on the project?'
Get examples

LISTEN
Suspend judgement
Don't evaluate

LEARN ABOUT FEELINGS
'What was it like working to a deadline?'

LISTEN
and reflect back

LEARN ABOUT MOTIVES
'What was it you liked about having responsibility?'

LISTEN

SUMMARISE AND SEEK AGREEMENT

START NEXT TOPIC WITH A GENERAL QUESTION
REPEAT SEQUENCE

66

Having asked your open question, the next thing to do is **listen to the response**.

> **It is the response that is important, not your next question. You do not have to worry about the next question, if you are listening to what the other person is saying. It will come automatically to you in response to their statement.**

(If you take nothing else away from reading this book, just practising this behaviour will increase your powers of understanding and perception dramatically.)

It is helpful at this stage to pick up and use the words that the other person is using, particularly emotive words and phrases like:

'I suppose I've been doing all right recently ...'.

The phrase 'all right' has a multitude of meanings, ranging from 'Absolutely brilliant' to 'Absolutely awful'. It is your role as counsellor to establish what the person means when they use that kind of phrase. Don't shy away from emotive words and phrases, they are the key to understanding your client.

Picking up on words used has a twofold effect: it allows you to understand the client's perspective and it enables you to show the client that you have been listening to them. This, in itself, will encourage them to talk further.

Having listened and heard what the client is saying, it is time for you to respond.

Responding

Elias Porter suggests that there are five categories of response:

> - **listening and understanding**
> - **probing**
> - **interpretive**
> - **evaluative**
> - **supportive.**

Listening and understanding

This kind of response is used to reassure the client that they are being heard and that the counsellor understands the client's point of view. For example:

> *'It sounds to me as though you are very determined about what you want to do.'*

Whilst this may sound like a passive thing to say, it is very important in terms of the individual feeling that what they are saying is both understood and accepted by the counsellor. Without these feelings, there can be no progression, as they will not feel 'safe' enough. It is a very constructive feeling to know that what you are saying is not regarded as trivial or silly.

Probing

This is a response which tries to elicit more information from the client, including things that they may not have thought of. For example:

> *'I wonder if you thought what effect that might have had on the rest of the team.'*

This kind of response, made at the wrong time, i.e. too early in the interview, can feel almost accusatory to the person, particularly if it is a closed question. It also takes some of the responsibility away from the individual, and almost puts the manager in an 'expert' position. This changes the dynamic of the conversation, and it may not encourage the client to feel they have a 'right' to say anything, i.e. they may feel inadequate. Probing responses do have a place later on in the interview, at the stage where it is helpful to the client to get a new perspective on the situation.

Interpretive

This is a response which implies an interpretation of the client's comments. For example:

69

'So that gave you a feeling of superiority.'

At this stage in the interview, you may not have the evidence to make this interpretation. You may sound, like this example, as though you are leading the client. Like the probing response, it may give the power to the counsellor: 'I know something you don't know ... Aren't I clever?' Again, this response is important later in the interview, when you have a great deal of evidence on which to base your interpretation, and it is necessary to move the client on.

Evaluative

This is a comment which judges what the client has said. For example:

'It would be a great shame if all your work on the project went to waste.'

This has the effect of potentially stopping them talking, as they may feel concerned that they are not saying the 'right' thing. It may even make the client feel angry and defensive. Again it may be useful at a later stage of the interview.

Supportive

This is sometimes a reflex action of the counsellor who feels the client needs an instant solution. For example:

> 'That must have been awful for you. What you need is a cup of tea and some tender loving care!'

This goes straight to a solution, without checking out the feelings of the client. It may be the wrong solution and implies that the counsellor knows best. (It may not have been awful!) It also implies that it can be easily sorted out and that the counsellor will do the sorting. It is verging on the advice-giving side, which is not counselling. It comes across as a sympathetic comment i.e. feeling *for* someone, rather than an empathic comment, which is feeling *with* someone. This again leaves the control with the counsellor, as opposed to the client, and takes away the client's involvement.

It is not that the listening and understanding response is the 'right' one every time, but more that if you introduce the other responses too early in the interview, they may stop the process.

Another important factor in giving the speaker every opportunity to speak is to use **Silence**. When you ask a question, wait for the answer. Silence does put a great deal of pressure on people to start talking. Make sure this pressure does not operate on you, and that you do not make the silence threatening. You are trying to give them time to think, not put them under pressure. Give them time to think through your question – the more penetrating the question, the more likely it is that the speaker will need a few moments to consider their reply. Silence is a little used, but very powerful, tool. If you do interrupt the speaker's thoughts, they will feel that you are not really interested in their reply and you will have lost contact.

Sometimes a silence can feel overpowering. At these times, it is necessary to ask yourself why it feels overpowering. Is it because you are uncomfortable with the silence? That is not a good reason for breaking it, and says more about you than the speaker. Is it because the speaker is uncomfortable with the silence? That is also not a good reason for breaking it, because it means you are ignoring the reason for their discomfort: i.e. something about the question or subject matter has made them feel uncomfortable. It is important that you establish exactly what that is and why it makes them uncomfortable. If a silence feels really impenetrable, it may be worth slightly rephrasing the question. If that still has no effect, it is sometimes helpful to challenge the silence by commenting on it, for example, 'Are you happy to continue thinking about it?'.

Silence is a little used, but very powerful, tool. If you do interrupt the speaker's thoughts, they will feel that you are not really interested in their reply and you will have lost contact.

71

Demonstrate interest in what is being said

One way of doing this is by using the funnel technique, and picking up on emotive words. Another way is by using **reflection**. This means taking what the speaker has said, paraphrasing it, and putting it back to the speaker. For example:

Client: Everything seemed to be very confused when we changed the planning system. Everyone was rushing around, without know ing what to do. We were all at a loss as to what we were supposed to be doing.

Manager: So the change in the planning system upset everyone in the department, including you. It seems as though you felt that you weren't getting any support or direction from anyone.

The object of this is to show the speaker what the listener has heard. This has a twofold effect:

1 It shows the speaker that you have been listening and, more importantly, you have understood what they have said.

2 It is a way of holding up to the speaker an image of themselves that they may not be aware they are projecting. By doing this, you are feeding back to the speaker information they can use when assessing their situation.

Reflection is not repeating parrot fashion what the speaker has said; this can be exceptionally irritating. It is taking what they have said and moving it on to its possible implications:

'When you described the new computer system as confusing, I got the impression that you were finding it difficult to understand.'

Another form of demonstrating interest and progressing the interview, is by the use of **summaries.** It is very encouraging to the speaker if the listener gives a short, accurate summary of what has been said. It helps the interaction by:

■ showing that the listener has really been paying attention to the speaker

■ providing the speaker with a chance to correct any misunderstandings

■ providing mutually acceptable milestones, from which the interview can progress.

If you don't understand, say so or ask for **clarification**. It is easy to feel that it is your fault if you do not understand. It may even cause you to resent the speaker for putting you in a potentially 'stupid' position. It is much more constructive to use phrases like:

'I'm not sure I understood that. Would you run through it again?'

Note the use of 'I'. It is important that if *you* do not understand, then you must own that feeling and not put it on to the speaker by saying things like 'You're not being very clear'. The use of the word 'I' gives the responsibility for the statement to the speaker, rather than the listener. This avoids the listener getting defensive, and avoiding the issue. It also makes it easier for them to accept their behaviour. This is because they are not being judged on their comments or actions, but rather, someone is making an observation. Managers, in their authoritative role, have a tendency to say things like 'You are being obstinate'. A manager/counsellor might say, 'I get the impression that you do not want to change your mind over this.'

73

Demonstrating interest is not just about responding verbally; it also covers non-verbal behaviour. It is not just receiving what the speaker says, but *how* they say it. Sometimes non-verbal communication may be used to replace language to express emotions, so the listener must **observe** as well as listen. Signs of attention include:

- eye contact (but not staring)
- appropriate smiling
- occasional nodding of encouragement (usually accompanied by 'semi-verbals' such as 'Uh huh', 'go on')
- attentive posture and position i.e. not too close, (but not too distant), leaning forward (but not aggressively).

Below are some of the variances you might encounter in the way people speak:

Speech dimension	*Characteristics*
VOLUME	Loudness, quietness, audibility
STRESS	Modulated, unmodulated
TONE	Admiring, disparaging
CLARITY	Clear enunciation, mumbling, slurring
PACE	Fast, slow, how easy is it to follow?

These variances might mean a number of things; for example, a drop to a very quiet voice might signify a shyness about that particular subject. Some people have naturally monotonous voices, so don't read too much into that! A great deal of the emotional content of what is being said, will be conveyed by vocal characteristics. 'He's a great help' might be either admiring or disparaging, depending on the way it is said.

Try saying, *He's* a great help
He's a *great* help
He's a great *help* using different tones and expressions ...

Body communication	*Characteristics*
PROXIMITY	Closeness, distance
POSTURE ORIENTATION	Facing, turning away, forwards, backwards
POSTURE	Tense, relaxed, rigid, slouched
FACIAL EXPRESSION	Animated, blank
EYE CONTACT	Staring, darting about, avoiding eye contact, seeking eye contact
GESTURE	Amount, variety, animated, helpless, aggressive

You need to be careful not to misinterpret non-verbal communication. The client sitting very stiffly, may have a bad back: they may not be defensively touching their nose, they may be about to sneeze! It is important to learn to interpret the behaviours, for example:

- Why are they avoiding eye contact?
- Is the subject matter threatening?
- Why are they leaning back in their chair?
- Are they bored, or distancing themselves from the question?

It is also important to match the body language to the words being spoken. For example, 'I am very happy in my job' spoken through clenched teeth with hands fidgeting is an 'incongruent' statement, i.e. the non-verbal behaviour does not match the words.

If you can perceive messages accurately, you are in a much better position to understand clients. (If in doubt, observe for longer, to see if it is a repeating pattern. Beware over-zealousness!)

Here are some obstacles to effective listening and some suggestions for improving listening:

Self-consciousness

If the listener is preoccupied with himself, or is over-concerned about the image they are creating, listening is likely to suffer.

Remember that you are not performing. It is the speaker who is your main concern. Anything that distracts you from what the speaker is saying will destroy the communication. **Concentrate on the speaker, not yourself.**

Daydreaming

The listener may get lost in their own thoughts and memories and the interaction is lost.

Concentrate! You can usually direct your attention where you wish. Effective listeners offer full and total concentration on the speaker. Recognise why you are daydreaming.

Emotional messages

The content of what the speaker is saying may arouse anger or hostility in the listener. The resulting emotions may block listening or cause a distortion of the message.

Be aware of your own feelings, and the reasons why the message content is so emotional for you. This will enable you to try to counteract the distortion to your understanding.

The long speech

The listener forgets the middle parts of long speeches, or loses track of the logic.

Don't be afraid to ask if you feel you are losing the thread. It is useful to summarise what you think you have heard and check that you have got it right so far. Ask for clarification if you are still confused.

The boring repetitive speech

The listener gets bored with what the speaker has to say, particularly as they seem to be repeating themselves.

Why are they repeating themselves? Is it because you have not heard them? You may need to tell them that they have already said that, but beware, in case you haven't heard exactly what they are saying. Check it out.

Reductive listening

The listener may modify the message received so that it sounds like previous messages. You tend to assume that people don't change.

Don't make assumptions about what is being, or what you think is going to be said. People are not consistent. They may change or say things which seem inconsistent to you. Ask the speaker to clarify.

77

Hearing what you want to hear

Your own motives and expectations lead you to assume that others share the same view. It may even lead you to premature conclusions and 'rigged evidence'.

Make a conscious effort to be aware of your motives and expectations. If the speaker only says what you would have expected them to say, then you have learned nothing from the conversation. Avoid premature conclusions about the client's problems.

'You agree with me'

The listener may modify what is heard to fit in with their own attitudes or opinions, screening out contrary information.

Don't be afraid to explore new or different perspectives. Having different ideas does not always lead to hostility or conflict – sometimes quite the reverse.

'You disagree with me'

The opposite also happens: that a listener feels hostility or infers that what is being said is against their own views.

Think about your feelings for the speaker, and try to distinguish them from your feelings about the message. Concentrate on the content of the message.

Evaluation

You tend to evaluate messages in terms of 'good/bad', 'right/wrong', etc. This clouds communication and if such evaluation is negative, may turn off the speaker.

It doesn't matter what your opinion is. Your role is to listen to the speaker, not to put your personal viewpoint across. Try not to evaluate, and focus on the speaker's right to their own views.

Rehearsing a reply

Part of the way through the message, the listener may start preparing a response, or another question, and become preoccupied. This will lose the message.

As soon as you want to start speaking, you are less effective as a listener. If you want the speaker to continue, stop rehearsing. You can give yourself time to respond after they have finished.

Environmental noise

External distractions can prevent message getting through.

Try to prevent distractions before they happen. If one does occur, remove it, or if this is not possible, reschedule or change location.

Having looked at enabling the client to 'tell the story', we need to look at ways of exploring and understanding the situation.

Stage Two – Understanding the situation

The counsellor helps the client to piece together the picture that has emerged in Stage One. They help them see broader issues and patterns where relevant, and so develop new perspectives on themselves and their situation. It also increases an awareness of the need for action.

In order to understand the situation, the counsellor needs the skills of:

> **STAGE ONE**
> - **confrontation**
> - **analysis**
> - **timing and pacing**
> - **lateral thinking**
> - **offering new perspectives.**

79

At this stage, the counsellor needs all the skills of Stage One. **You don't ever stop listening or observing in a counselling session**. You are continuing to observe and listen, but are now ready to take the process a stage further.

The individual is starting to talk and by now you should be getting a good idea of what the situation is. It may not be the one you thought it would be. It may not be the situation the client thought it would be. Frequently, someone will be referred to you for what appears to be a valid reason. Don't try and deal with that reason until you have established whether it is the true issue (see the example below).

Case study

Jonathan came to see his manager because he felt that his time man-agement was poor and he wanted to go on a course. The 'presenting problem' was Jonathan's 'poor' time management. On discussing the matter further, it appeared that Jonathan had plenty of time to do the tasks he was supposed to do. However, he was not sure how to do them and no one had shown him how. Therefore the real problem was not one of time management, but a question of assessing Jonathan's skills, and their relation to the job he was supposed to be doing.

Problems often arise when counsellors get lost in the detail of the story and, in doing so, lose both the message and the person.

So what do you need to look for when you are listening to a person's story?

What you need is a **DRAWING** of the person:

D	**Description of self:** Clients are not aware of how they describe themselves. They frequently use recurring themes, words and phrases in their 'stories', for example, conflict. It is these scenarios that give the counsellor an insight into the client's self-perception.
R	**Role:** How do people view themselves when they tell you their story? Are they active or passive? Do they seek or take responsibility? Do they see everything as happening to them? Do they accept blame, or do they consistently put the blame outside of themselves?
A	**Attitude:** What kind of feelings do they have about the difficulty they are facing? Are they hopeful or despairing? Do they feel betrayed, lost or do they have some central reserve of confidence that they can build on to comfort themselves with?
W	the **Way the story is told:** This is a key element of counselling; the tone in which the story is told is the most significant source of insight for the counsellor. The client might be describing a trivial or important incident, but how are they relaying it? Are they telling it in a depressed, tired, don't care way? Is there anger bubbling behind their words? Is there a feeling of a loss or gain of power behind this simple story? Why have they chosen this particular story? The counsellor's response should be not to the details of the story, but to the underlying tone which gives the story its meaning.
I	**Interested parties:** Who is involved in the story? Are there recurring characters, or characters with similar behaviours and effects? How do they relate to the client? How does the client feel about them?
N	**Nature of the conflict:** What is the nature of the conflict? How does it show itself? Is it a recurring conflict in other situations, in or out of work? What is at the heart of the conflict?

81

G **Going over it:** Have you heard this story before? Were you listening before, or is the client trying to underline a point? It may not be the same story in its details, but are the theme and conflict the same? Clients repeat stories because they feel the counsellor hasn't heard, or is not giving enough emphasis to the particular point they are trying to make.

Managing the process

Summary

An important part of Stage Two, 'Understanding the problem', is the ability to recognise when an individual needs to be brought face to face with some issues that they have been avoiding. Without the counsellor doing this, the client will be unable to move on.

It means being able to recognise and understand defences and being able to point them out without destroying them. It means confronting and feeding back descriptions of behaviour. It is also necessary to challenge the 'games' people use to avoid dealing with issues, both wittingly and unwittingly. Once you are dealing with the real issues you can begin to analyse them and look at their implications before moving on to the next stage. A good manager/counsellor needs to be aware of situations where confrontation is called for, well versed in the skills of confrontation, and assertive enough to use them.

The main skills for the counsellor to use are:

- **an understanding of defence mechanisms and how they operate**
- **recognising and being able to resist 'games'**
- **the skills of confronting and giving feedback.**

Confronting literally means bringing someone face to face with what is happening and what they are doing. This involves accurate, objective and specific descriptions of what is happening.

Dealing with distractions

Sometimes at this stage of the session, you may feel that the drawing does not quite fit together. It may be helpful to ask yourself, 'I could move the client on, if I understood ...'. When you can finish the sentence, you can progress the client on. It is breaking down what the blocks to understanding are that is crucial to getting the story straight, and identifying the true issues, not just the 'presenting' ones. Only then can you help the client to deal with the issues. At this stage, a sense of timing is crucial. If you interrupt the client, you may prevent them telling the story in the terms they want to use. If you wait too long to respond, the client may perceive you as passive or disinterested. There is a rhythm to telling and understanding the story, which allows for the counsellor's intervention. Clients almost always provide the necessary breaks to do this. You, as a counsellor, have to listen for them.

Sometimes, when you or the client are facing an issue which is uncomfortable, or you feel you might be put in a position where you feel vulnerable, your first reaction will be to avoid it. This is done in many subtle ways, but the basic aim is always the same; avoid the potentially threatening issue. Frequently, people do not know they are doing this; it may be an instinctive defensive reaction.

The defended self

Through the processes of growing and trying out different experiences, individuals develop a set of ideas about themselves. They will have an idea about the sort of person they are, in each of their social roles: as a parent, as a spouse, as a manager, as a team player etc. They will also have an ideal view of themselves; of the sort of person they feel they ought, or would like, to be. This ideal view also covers their values, dreams and fantasies about themselves and their place in society. This set of ideas is known collectively as the **'self concept'**.

The self concept

One definition of being 'emotionally mature', is the process of developing a realistic self concept. This is one in which the person's view of themselves is largely in agreement with other people's view of them. Many emotional and psychological problems have their roots in an unrealistic or inappropriate self concept. The individual is likely to be quite open in discussing some aspects of the self concept. For example, when someone says, 'I've never thought of myself as the sporty type' or 'I've always thought of myself as a very approachable person'.

However, other aspects of the self concept will be totally private. In fact, they are the most private of all possessions (the very top of the communications pyramid). These aspects, which are likely to be of central importance, are never discussed, even with those close to them and certainly not with work colleagues. Individuals guard the concept of themselves most carefully of all, because the self concept is them.

Defence mechanisms

The individual develops a range of devices with which to guard themselves from criticism. These are defence mechanisms.

Typical defences include:

- Denial, or rejection of information, e.g. 'That's just not true. I'm never like that.'
- Blaming others, 'circumstances beyond our control', or the weather, e.g. 'It wasn't my fault. They all left me with it.'
- Lying, e.g. 'He never gave me any information about it.'
- Agreeing quickly, e.g. 'Oh, that's absolutely right. I'll try it your way tomorrow.'
- Changing the subject, e.g. 'Well, it's not getting the contract that's important. It's the fact that I wasn't told about the change of plan.'

There are many more, and some come in a combination.

There is no one reason why people use particular mechanisms at particular times. It seems that each person discovers and then develops those defences which work for them personally, in different situations.

In some cultures, feedback is relatively easily accepted. For example, in Australia, it is not unusual for strangers or slight acquaintances to make personal comments. In a culture of privacy, like Britain, feedback is rarely given and even praise is received defensively. 'Oh, it was nothing really. Anyone could have done it.' Feedback creates an awareness of the need for change. This implies, particularly to the British, that the individual is somehow inadequate for failing to spot the need themselves. This leads to a feeling of guilt, and then to defensiveness.

It is very difficult to know how central a particular piece of behaviour is to a person's self concept. Apparently trivial behaviours can represent key themes. For example, a scruffy appearance may simply reflect that you did not know anyone minded about it, or it may imply a deep seated concern to be seen as creative, individual and independent. A constant 'devil may care' attitude may indicate a very deep concern to do the 'right' thing.

If a behaviour is important, it is likely to be highly defended.

The pattern of defence that people use is not accidental, neither is it just throwing up obstacles to keep the counsellor at bay. The style of the defence will tell you a great deal about the individual. (The style of your response will tell you a great deal about yourself.) It is an insightful and descriptive language that counsellors need to translate and understand, rather than try to get rid of a defence in an irritated way. Counselling is not a situation in which the counsellor can 'win'. When it feels like that, it means that you are as defensive as the client, and must prove yourself by 'conquering' the client.

Apparently trivial behaviours can represent key themes. For example, a scruffy appearance may simply reflect that you did not know anyone minded about it, or it may imply a deep seated concern to be seen as creative, individual and independent.

The counsellor needs to evaluate the client's defence mechanisms, before dealing with them:

- How long have they been there?
- What happened to challenge the defence mechanisms and bring them up at this stage?

- How much does this person need them in order to function 'normally' at this moment in time?
- If the defences are not working as well as they have done in the past, why is this?
- Is this a sign that their ability to cope is lessening, or are they getting closer to an important insight into themselves?
- What kind of defences do people use?

Intellectualisation

This defence is about being able to think about the problems in an abstract way, and talk about them theoretically. Somehow, this keeps the problem 'out there' rather than within the person. In this way clients need feel no emotion, and can talk on and on. They often use psychological terminology, and whilst it may sound as though the client is talking about significant subjects, they are avoiding themselves, which is the main issue.

You will probably have to point out to the client the way in which they are using this defence. You do *not* do this by saying, 'Do you realise that you are using an intellectual defence to avoid telling the truth about yourself?' This is answering the client in kind. A more appropriate response would be one that reflected the counsellor's own state of mind, at that moment in the relationship. This is usually a feeling of being kept on the outside, or at arm's length from the client. So you might say, 'We seem to be talking a lot, but don't appear to be getting very far.' Or, 'I understand what you are saying, but I don't get any feeling of you being involved in the situation.'

Expressing irritation

When a counsellor gets a little too close to the source of the problem, clients frequently respond by getting irritable. This can deflect the counsellor by making *them* angry, thus throwing them off the scent of the client's issues. It is essential that the counsellor responds to the person rather than to the defensive attack. 'It sounds as though this is a difficult subject for you to discuss,' might be the kind of response that would be appropriate in this case. This is taking the conversation back to the client and away from the counsellor.

Diverting

Another method of avoiding an issue is to either change or divert the subject, or launch into irrelevant detail that confuses the counsellor. The only thing to do here is to bring the client back, by using phrases like: 'That's certainly true. I feel that we are getting away from the point. Can we just go back to ...'.

89

Confrontation and dealing with game playing

In order to get past the defences to deal with the real issues, the counsellor will have to confront the client. Confrontation is not a heavy stick to beat people with. The counsellor needs to understand why they are confronting, and ensure that they are not using it as a way of showing up other people's weaknesses, and thereby their own superiority. Confrontation is used to point out the defences, not destroy them. It is very easy to feel hostile towards a client who is provoking you, or leading you off the track. It is sometimes even satisfying to respond in a hostile way. However, a hostile response means that you are no longer counselling. You have entered into a 'game' with the client, and your responding in this way will ensure their control. This is neither confrontation, nor is it constructive.

Sometimes the 'gameplaying' is actually the problem itself. This 'gameplaying' is usually started by the client (although not always). If the counsellor does not recognise it and deal with it, there will be no constructive result to the discussion. There will be many times when the counsellor is drawn into the 'game', for many reasons. This is called **'colluding'**. In order to stop the 'game', the counsellor will have to confront the client. **Confronting does not mean aggression**.

If people become comfortable with their delusions they will try to hang on to them. They may get their satisfaction by playing games in the interview, or outside the interview. Eric Berne's theory of transactional analysis suggested that if people got what they wanted from playing games, they would obviously continue to play them. He suggested that people often wrote themselves 'scripts'. Like a play, these are a series of actions and sentences which form a familiar response system for them. These scripts are patterns of behaviour that affect the way people act in their personal life, and what they do and say on the job. They may follow patterns, such as always fumbling, never quite making it, getting to the top, getting put down, getting things their way, putting others down, always striving, etc.

People get used to reacting in a particular way, and sometimes it may be part of the counsellor's role to point this out to the client. The number of games people can play to avoid dealing with life is endless. Here are some descriptions of the games most commonly found in organisational settings.

Sometimes the initiator of the game will set up or observe a situation where somebody makes a mistake, only to step in at a later stage to triumphantly point out the error. They are doing this to give themselves a feeling of superiority and, by putting someone else down, they feel good about themselves, i.e. more powerful.

There is a game where the player, by constantly misunderstanding directives or information, convinces themselves of their own lack of intelligence. This game is clearly recognised, for they are the people who constantly misunderstand when everyone else understands most clearly. These people do not want to feel powerful and good about themselves, quite the reverse. They want to feel 'not OK', and use this game to avoid facing up to themselves. At some stage in the game they are likely to say 'I must be stupid'. Their aim is to make you say that they are.

Another way the initiator might try to ensure they feel 'OK' about themselves, is to ask for solutions to a problem they pose. As each solution is prefaced by the remark 'Why don't you ...?', the game player is always able to counter with the argument 'Yes, but ...', followed by a rejection of the idea. The more you try to offer ideas, the more powerful they feel and the more frustrated you feel. This game is frequently played at meetings and counselling sessions (and is yet another good reason for not telling the client what to do).

91

If these games are a way of avoiding dealing with life, then it is important that the counsellor challenges them by feeding back to the client what they are doing. The feedback should be given in a way that the client will accept! For example, they are unlikely to accept derogatory words like, 'You're manipulative' or 'That's being selfish'. If you want to tell the client that they are being manipulative, you have to describe the behaviours involved, without judging them. A value judgement would immediately invite either a denial, or a game from the client.

This means that you need to **describe the situation and behaviours in a specific way**. If, for example, you wanted to tell a client that you felt that they were selfish, you must describe the kind of things the client has done to lead you to this conclusion. For example, 'You have mentioned on several occasions that when people are discussing things you are not interested in, you switch off. You have described your impatience with members of staff who do not understand what you say the first time you say it.' These are descriptions of the person's behaviour.

It also helps to describe what happens as a result of their behaviour. For example, how other people are affected by their behaviour:

Counsellor: What do you think you do that upsets the team?

Client: Well, I do demand a very high standard of neatness in their work and I can't abide sloppy dressers. I always tell them, as soon as they walk in the door.

The purpose of giving the feedback is to show the client what they are doing, and help them understand its impact on others.

Confrontation is not meant to be a personal exchange. It does not end with the counsellor identifying or exposing the defence or defensive behaviour of the client.

> **Confronting literally means bringing someone face to face with what is happening and what they are doing. This involves accurate, objective and specific descriptions of what is happening.**

This step is the beginning of the process of working with the real issues, as opposed to the presenting problem. Before a manager can hope to progress a member of their team, they need to be sure that they are dealing with the real issue. Challenging is a key part of the manager's role in developing staff, but it is all too often avoided; not sincerely for the sake of the 'client', but for the sake of the manager, who feels uncomfortable. It therefore becomes a developmental issue for the manager.

If the counselling process is used appropriately, it not only improves the performance of the client, but also the manager.

7

Taking it forward

Summary

This is potentially the most challenging stage in the interview process, and the one where the counsellor is most active. It is also the one which will be seen as having the most importance to the organisation, as it is about results. The counsellor needs to identify and agree on a course of action for the client and help them plan ways of implementing it. They also need to look at some of the issues that can stop the client achieving their goals.

The counsellor needs the skills of:

- **analysis and problem solving**
- **feedback**
- **a knowledge of resources**
- **goal setting**
- **helping clients assess strategies and choose appropriately**
- **helping the client draw up realistic plans**
- **supporting and maintaining the client through implementation.**

Moving on

This is the third stage in the counselling process. Having got the story, and explored and understood the situation, you are ready to move on to the final stage.

Developing strategies and gaining acceptance

The counsellor aims to help the client to act, based on their new understanding of themselves and their situation. The client and counsellor agree on a course of action. The counsellor explores with the client a variety of ways of achieving the goals that have been set, and helps them identify what resources and strengths they have and can use. They help the client choose and work out for themselves a specific plan of action, taking into account costs to themselves and others. The counsellor supports the client in implementing their plan, and helps them evaluate the results.

In order to move on, the counsellor needs:

- **all the skills of Stages One and Two**
- **objective and goal setting**
- **to use creative thinking and problem solving techniques**
- **to encourage and support**
- **a knowledge of resources**
- **a knowledge of how behaviour is changed and**

The counsellor is most active, in terms of their input, during this stage. However, the fundamental principle of letting the client solve their own problem is still paramount.

In terms of the organisation, this is the most important stage: the action stage. The manager as counsellor is balancing on the fence between their client's needs and the organisation's needs. The organisation may not be able to give the client the time to pace or direct themselves.

The counsellor's experience at Stage Three may be greater than the client's, and the skill required at this stage, is one of imparting the knowledge without telling the client what to do. The first thing the counsellor and client must agree, is the direction that the client needs to take: which **goals** to aim for.

Goal setting

Everything in Stages One and Two is preparatory to this:

95

- explore and clarify the client's situation
- focus on and identify the problem(s)
- reflect to the client new perspectives
- set goals and directions.

Goal setting completes the process. Everything done after the goal process, for example, choosing strategies and implementing action plans, is done to ensure that the goals are met. The real challenge of counselling, for some, does not lie in the identification of problem situations, it is frequently found in the *management* of these situations. Sometimes clients (and counsellors!) want to skip the goal setting process once they have identified the problem. They just want to deal with it immediately. Sometimes the converse is true, problems can make the client feel shut off and overwhelmed.

A goal helps to keep the client (and the counsellor) achievement oriented. It helps them to picture themselves managing the situation. Clear goals:

> - **focus the client's attention on action**
> - **motivate the client to look for strategies**
> - **give clients a reason to persevere.**

GUIDELINES FOR GOAL SETTING

S   **Specific**
M   **Measurable**
A   **Activity and achievement based**
R   **Realistic**
T   **Timed**

Smart people know exactly what they are trying to achieve.

Specific

Vague goals allow you to put them off. For example, 'My New Year resolution is to get in shape this year.' Such vague aims are wishes rather than goals.

> **A goal is a statement of what you want to do and how you want to do it.**

It is sometimes helpful to have an aim, and then translate the aim into a specific outcome. For example:

Aim: I really want to understand my team better, and be able to delegate more work.

Goal: Over the next three meetings, I am going to delegate the chair to different members of the team. I will observe, discuss and give them feedback on how they did.

Aim: I want to get myself in physical shape.

Goal: Within six months, I will be running four miles in under 50 minutes, at least three times a week.

In both these cases, a particular behaviour is being described. In the latter, a pattern is established and consistently pursued.

Measurable

You must be able to tell whether you have achieved your goal or not. Without this knowledge, you feel no accomplishment. You cannot know if you are making progress, if you don't know where you started.

'I want to cut out time wasting in meetings' is not measurable.

'By the end of the month, I will have had two meetings, lasting no longer than two hours each' is measurable.

It is not always necessary to include numbers in order to measure progress, but some quantifier is necessary.

Activity and achievement based

The achievements of the goals are not the way to get there. They are what will have been accomplished or achieved at the end. For example, 'I need to get some training in interpersonal skills' is a method rather than an achievement. The goal is only achieved when you have gained, practised and actually used those skills in interpersonal situations.

Gerard Egan suggests using the 'past participle' approach; for example, skills *acquired*, drinking *stopped*, number of meetings *decreased*.

It is about knowing what you want from the method, as an outcome, rather than what the method consists of, i.e. what you want to get at the end of it.

Realistic

A goal is realistic if:

- the client has the resources necessary to achieve the goal
- there are no external circumstances preventing them achieving the goal
- the cost of achieving it is not too high.

> 'Nothing breeds success like success. Conversely, nothing causes feelings of despair like personal failure. A primary principle of goal setting is to measure the motivation level of the individual. But goal setting can have precisely the opposite effect if it produces a yardstick that constantly makes the individual feel inadequate.'[1]

Clients can sabotage their efforts if they choose goals that are beyond their reach or which include resources that are beyond their control. For example, Steven wants to move into the training department of his organisation. However, there are no vacancies at present and the department is, in fact, shedding staff. Therefore it would not be a good idea for Steven to set a goal that involved moving into the training department, as he will be unable to influence its result.

It is also important that the goals are the client's goals, and not the counsellor's.

Carl Rogers, in a film of a counselling session (Rogers, Perl and Ellis 1965), is asked by a client what she should do about her relationship with her daughter. He says, 'I think you have been telling me all along what you want to do.' The client actually knew what she wanted to do; what she wanted from the counsellor was not his suggestions, but his *approval* for what she wanted to do. If he had given her his approval, the goal would have become his goal, instead of hers. At another point in the interview he asks, 'What is it that you want me to tell you to do?'

This puts the responsibility for the goal setting back where it belongs – with the client.

Timed

Like vague and non-specific goals, those that are to be done 'sometime or other', or with no time frame, never seem to get done. If an individual says, 'I am going to set aside three hours a week to organise my staff group, as soon as this current rush is over', they are unlikely to achieve the goal, because the time frame is not clear. It is almost like paying 'lip service' to the idea of a goal, without ever really intending to achieve it.

For a goal to be achieved, it must meet all of the **SMART** rules. If any one component is missing, it could be the element that stops the person dealing with the problem.

99

Attaining goals

Having defined the goals, you can move on to identify how to attain them. There are three stages to this process:

- **identifying and assessing strategies**
- **helping clients put together a plan of action**
- **helping clients to implement the plans.**

Identifying and assessing strategies

Strategy is the art of identifying and choosing realistic methods of achieving goals. It also means looking at ways of getting round problems that may arise.

What sort of issues prevent people from solving problems?

- **Reliance on authority giving them the answers:** People come to the counsellor expecting the right answer, and may sometimes block efforts to help them by playing games like 'Yes but ...'.
- **Fear:** Clients are often fearful of suggesting ideas that might sound stupid, and their anxiety about the problem gets in the way of them dealing with it.
- **Long-term habits:** Some individuals have deeply ingrained behaviour patterns, and as such are resistant to change.
- **Long stay problem:** The problem has been around a long time, and the person still has no idea of how to deal with it.

There are a number of ways the counsellor can help the client break the block that is stopping them developing strategies. Some of the problems arise because it is very easy to get caught in the trap of only seeing things in one dimension. For example, if you were shown a rubber tyre and asked how many uses you could find for it, your initial thoughts would be centred around what you know to be the 'normal' uses of a tyre, i.e. put it on a car. Your list would be very short and then you would become 'blocked'. This is because if you only view things in one light, you tend to evaluate any problems associated with it in the same one light. Your mind screens off anything outside of that dimension. This is called 'convergent thinking'. It partly stems from school, where you are encouraged to give only 'right' answers ('wrong' or creative answers are not rewarded and are usually ignored or punished) and therefore learn to evaluate everything before saying anything.

However, many problems in life are too complex for 'convergent thinking', and you need more perspectives . This is known as 'divergent thinking'. But it is difficult to do this, because you are so programmed to think in a straight line.

One way of getting round this, is to use a technique called

'brainstorming'. Brainstorming is a technique for generating ideas, possibilities and alternative courses of action. The objective is to identify as many ideas as possible. When you brainstorm, you write down anything you think of, without evaluating it first. That means you write it down, however silly it sounds. So if you go back to the tyre example, you could find yourself writing things like 'hula hoop, necklace, boat ...'. Some of these suggestions are silly, but don't evaluate them until you have got as many thoughts as you can in five minutes.

When you brainstorm, you write down anything you think of, without evaluating it first. That means you write it down, however silly it sounds.

101

If you use this technique when you are trying to help clients identify possible strategies for achieving goals, it is very important that they do not criticise the ideas they are generating, at the initial stages. Suspending judgement in this way also helps avoid the client playing 'Yes, but ...'. So don't say things like 'Explain what you mean', or 'I'm not sure I like that idea'. Even the craziest possibilities may have the kernel of an idea in them. The more ideas they develop, the more likelihood there is of finding one that will work. When you have all the ideas, then it helps for the counsellor to clarify some before evaluating. For example:

Client: I suppose there might be the possibility of a transfer.

Counsellor: Are there different types of transfer available at the moment?

This is still leaving the problem with the client, but helping them to clarify ideas often leads to new possibilities. After this process, you can begin to evaluate the ideas you have in relation to the problem and the resources the client has. (Skills, knowledge, emotional resources.) It is helpful to analyse potential strategies in terms of potential benefits and potential losses, and the acceptability or unacceptability of the benefits or losses.

Helping clients put together a plan of action

Some strategies are quite simple and their achievement method is very obvious. Others are more complicated and demand the client working out a step by step procedure for achieving their goals. When helping the client formulate a plan of action, it is useful to use the same guidelines as those for goal setting. When they formulate their action plans, they often come up against some of the problems they will face in implementing them. It is part of the counsellor's role to help the client deal with the obstacles, and not avoid them or be deterred from carrying on. Many clients will, however, make decisions based on impulse and bias, rather than a logical thought procedure. It is important for counsellors to remind themselves of their non-directive role, i.e. it is the client's decision and, while you can point out various issues, at the end of the day, you cannot *make* them do anything.

Some clients have a clear idea of what they are going to do, and are ready to walk out of the session at this point – all they want to do is get started. Others may need support and maintenance to implement their plans. If their plan fails or comes to a halt, or the client becomes overcome by inertia, it may fall to the counsellor to facilitate the client.

Helping the client to implement their plans is a part of the counselling role that is often forgotten because, in many professional counselling cases, a plan might not be appropriate. However, it is particularly relevant to managers counselling internally. This is because it is about **results in the workplace**.

Helping clients to implement the plans

When a plan does not work or falls apart, it is helpful to be able to understand and analyse what has made it do so. Kurt Lewin, in his forcefield theory, said that there were two forces to analyse when problem solving: those that stop you from achieving your goals and those that help you. It is also useful for the counsellor to give the client feedback about how they have perceived them implementing their plans. Again, this particularly applies to counselling in the workplace, and it is part of the manager's role to observe a client's progress. (It might be important to build this 'monitoring' dimension into the contract.)

103

Case study

Alan Brown was a very bright, articulate, capable manager. He had a reputation for very high quality work, almost to the point of obsession. He had just taken over the role of team manager in an information technology department of a large company. He had a team of committed individuals who were technically good and always brought projects in to time, but only just. Alan was feeling very overloaded by the amount of work and the time pressures he felt under. He respected and admired his manager but felt he was getting little support from him although the manager relied heavily on Alan. He was completely exhausted trying to do everything and was beginning to be very short tempered with his staff.

Alan's manager eventually called him in to his office, and they came to the conclusion that Alan wasn't delegating enough of his work and had taken on a role that was inappropriate. Together they came up with some goals and an action plan to enable Alan to 'let go' of some of his jobs, and use his time more efficiently. Alan went away, initially satisfied, but when it came to implementing his plan, he found it difficult to put in any of his new structure as his boss kept giving him new projects and appeared to have forgotten their discussion. They met again and tried to analyse what was stopping Alan from achieving his goals. They analysed the situation as follows:

Things that were stopping Alan achieve his goals	**Things that were helping Alan achieve his goals**
His manager was continually giving him work when he already had far too much.	His manager was genuinely concerned for Alan and respected his skills and abilities.
Alan did not feel his work was valued by his manager, and therefore he was tentative about instigating new procedures.	His manager wanted the same final achievement as Alan.
Alan's manager was not quite sure of his role and therefore was interfering with Alan.	Alan was very highly motivated to put in new structures, in order to delegate appropriately and free his time.
	The team was very supportive of Alan and endorsed his plans for reorganisation.

Once they had analysed it in this way, it was very easy to work on the issues that were preventing Alan using some of the things that were helping him. So, for example, they sorted out the misunderstandings that were occurring between Alan and his manager.

Some people may balk at the idea of such a mechanistic approach to goal setting and problem solving: it may not be appropriate for all clients. Like all the techniques we have described in this book, it is an approach to be considered and adapted to the situation, rather than rigidly followed.

Having established a plan of action with the client, it is time for you to end the session. Many inexperienced counsellors underestimate the importance of ending a session professionally. If the ending does not refer back to the initial contract, it will be difficult to see what has been achieved. If there is no explicit end to the interview, the client (and the counsellor) can feel uncomfortable.

If you have set your contract at the beginning of the session, it is easy to terminate when you agreed to. Most experienced counsellors restrict time for various reasons:

- needing to be on time for other appointments
- training clients to understand limits of time, so that they can use the time in the session to full effect
- putting a very tangible end to the process makes it more 'secure' for the client
- it prevents a professional contact becoming a personal one.

105

However, there may be emergencies which justify the occasional deviation from ending on time. Professional counsellors pace their session so that things are leading up to the end. When you are counselling as a manager, it is more likely that when the time you have set is nearly up, you will have to summarise and say something like, 'Well, we have about five minutes to go ...' and maybe add a tentative question, if appropriate, 'I'm wondering whether there is anything further you would like to bring up before we finish.'

When starting out counselling, some counsellors are not assertive enough when finishing off their sessions. Sometimes they let them drift on or finish the session in such a way that the client perceives it as a lack of interest. It is quite helpful to refer back to the contract and the agreed perceived outcomes and expectations. This helps to give a structured, 'rounded-off' feel to both the client and counsellor, about where you have come from and what you have achieved. In that light, it is also useful to sum up the action points and do a final recap. For example, 'So we have agreed that you will keep a log of all your activities this week. We will meet again next Tuesday at three o'clock, for an hour, when we will analyse the implications of your log in terms of you managing your time and delegating more tasks. Is that OK?'

One more issue which needs to be addressed is the issue of keeping notes and records. Some counsellors take copious notes throughout the sessions, others make notes at the end of the interview. Some do not take notes at all. The normal reason people give for taking notes is that they might forget things that are said.

Some counsellors are not assertive enough when finishing off their sessions. Sometimes they let them drift on or finish the session in such a way that the client perceives it as a lack of interest.

It is important to establish the purpose of the notes. Are they for the counsellor or the client? What will happen to them at the end of the session? Are they to establish progress against goals set? Are they for analysis, to help plan other ways of thinking?

If you listen and summarise carefully, you will not forget things because you will be constantly updating the flow. Of course, you might miss the odd word, but that needs to be balanced against the effect note taking has on the interview:

- it disturbs the flow because you lose eye contact
- it can be threatening to the client because they cannot see what you are writing. This will affect their willingness to speak
- it distracts the client, and may make them (and/or the counsellor) lose their train of thought.

Bearing these points in mind, can your note taking wait, or is it necessary? What will you do with the notes? Will the client feel happy with a written record, however informal? How does it affect confidentiality? You need to consider these questions before making a decision. If you do decide to take notes, ensure that you tell the client, and explain your reasons and what will happen to the notes in order to reassure them of your motives.

Ending the first or fifth session with an individual is not an end in itself. If the manager has taken the role of guide and facilitator, then they need to review progress with the individual on a regular basis, even if it is only for five minutes a week.

It is difficult for results oriented managers to walk this delicate tightrope of providing support and letting go, but the rewards for the individual, manager and the organisation, in terms of maximising their people power, are enormous.

Reference

[1] Locke, E. A. and Latham, G. P., *Goal Setting: a motivational technique that works*. Prentice Hall 1984

The greatest thing in the world is to know how to belong to ourselves.

MONTAIGNE

8

Understanding the counsellor in the process

Summary

The manager/counsellor stands to learn and develop almost as much as the client during the counselling process. They can only do this, and deal appropriately with the client, if they are aware of the issues that affect the counsellor. The two major threats to the counsellor come from insufficient self-awareness and confusing their own personal issues with those of the client. If the counsellor is not aware of their own feelings, they will find it difficult to be objective with a client, and distinguish their own feelings from the client's. Not only do you have to concentrate on, and listen to the client, you have to know yourself.

Potential issues are:

- **insufficient self-awareness**
- **threats to self-esteem**
- **limits of ability**
- **personal attacks**
- **confusing personal issues with clients**
- **identifying with the client**
- **projection**
- **transference**
- **letting go**
- **dealing with the client's emotional dependency**

Your feelings as a counsellor

If effective interpersonal helping is always tied to the relationship with the other person, then you must focus on yourself, as you are when you are with that person. You often think that if you get enough information about the other person, this is enough. This is crucial to understanding their situation, but you also have to take into consideration yourself and your own reactions. This is the demanding double focus that is essential for counselling.

The potential stress of unrecognised and unmanaged personal involvement is very strong. As a counsellor, you have to know who you are and why you react in the way you do.

You must know what is taking place inside yourself as well as inside others. These feelings are sometimes interrelated. The potential stress of unrecognised and unmanaged personal involvement is very strong. As a counsellor, you have to know who you are and why you react in the way you do. Those who do not understand themselves, or what is happening in the course of the process, can easily get lost. This is *not* because the client has such complex problems, but because the counsellor has not learned to take their own situation into account.

So there are two issues:

- not being able to deal with the problem, because your personal issues prevent you and you realise this
- not being able to deal with the problem, and not knowing why.

It is better to understand some of the issues or dynamics of the 'helping' situation. To remain empathic (understanding what someone is saying and its implications), demands both a sense of yourself and a sense of the client. It begins with the very base line of listening to the client. This is not the same as waiting for another person to finish before you start talking. Nor does it mean daydreaming while someone tells what you consider to be a very familiar story. It means giving up your own thoughts and interests for a while, in order to be able to give your complete attention to the other person. They tell you *that* something is going on, and they give you major clues as to *what* is going on. Listening for, and interpreting, these clues provides you with the answer to whether you will be able to be of any help to the client.

These considerations lead us on to the feelings you experience as a counsellor, and the effect they have on both your reactions and those of the client. (Try to ignore the use of jargon and concentrate on understanding ideas that are not complicated, but extremely important. They describe some of the processes that go on in the enabling or empowering relationship.)

Let us first look at those feelings the person you are helping seems to have towards you in the counselling relationship. They are feelings which are appropriate to previous significant figures in their lives. This could include parents, or those who took their place. These feelings are present all the time, but they are more pronounced in the counselling relationship. In a professional counselling situation, this is a very important stage of the process. In terms of counselling in the workplace, it may manifest itself in a more dilute form: this might mean that feelings towards the organisation or bosses might be shown in the client's behaviour towards you in the interview. These feelings could be either positive or negative. Counsellors should be aware that this can happen. They should not feel that the person feels this way towards them personally.

For example, if the individual has had a promotion knocked by

111

company restructuring and is feeling very anti-company, they may express their anger at the counsellor, because it is a channel that has presented itself. If the counsellor takes this personally, they are not listening to what the client is saying. They are not angry with *you*, and the problem is not *you*. The problem is with the client's feelings towards the organisation. It is this issue that you have to deal with.

These feelings are a dilute form of what is called, in a therapeutic counselling process, **transference**.

The other side of this process are the feelings you have for the individual whom you are counselling. These feelings may include feelings of being strongly attracted to, or unattracted to, the person. There is nothing wrong with having these feelings about people. A problem only arises when you avoid acknowledging the feelings because they arouse in you feelings of surprise, shame or guilt. You have to identify these feelings, in order to understand and help your client.

These feelings are similar to the process of **countertransference** in the therapeutic counselling process.

For example, a male manager might find himself attracted to a female member of staff he is interviewing. Defensive about himself, he does not admit these reactions and only expresses them indirectly. He treats the woman harshly and antagonises her frequently. This is not because of anything she has said or done, but in response to his own subconscious feelings of attraction to her. He has established distance from her in a destructive way, in order to handle his own feelings. The irony of the situation is that although he does not acknowledge these feelings, they dominate the relationship anyway and prevent him understanding the client.

At this point, it might be helpful to list a few '**Do nots**':

1 **Do not panic:** The calmer you are, the more likely you are to hear the signals coming from your client as well as from yourself. The key to this, is being patient and developing a willingness to suspend action, until you have a fairly good idea of the sources and nature of their reaction and your own.

2 **Do not misinterpret:** Try not to leap in, which is the easiest thing to do in a situation where you feel out of control. This generally makes things worse for both you and the client. It is worth mentally sitting back and letting things become clear to the client. If you listen carefully, the meaning will become clearer. (If you feel that is too simplistic, try it. It is astonishing how the quality of listening and hearing can enlarge your vision of a situation.)

3 **Do not force reactions:** Do not try to artificially change either your reactions or those of the client. Instead of covering emotional tracks, you should learn from them. You may not always react the way you would like, or in a manner you consider ideal, but in the same way that you look at a clients' reactions to help define their situation, **the way you react defines you**. The way you react may not be appropriate, but you have to be aware of it and acknowledge it. You will lose your way only when you do not acknowledge your feelings.

When you reach the stage in the interview where you are empathising and getting close to your client, it is crucial that you remain separate, in order to avoid an **identification** with the client. At this stage you are trying to **get into their head while remaining in yours**. If, however, you get too close to the client and 'identify' with them, i.e. you want to solve their problem yourself, you are no longer operating objectively from your head, but are seeing things from inside their head only. While you are in their head, you cannot help them, because you are in the same position as they are. In order to help a client effect

113

change, you have to remain 'in *your* head'.

Remaining objective, or 'in your head', is not the same as being distant. It means recognising and respecting your own individuality, as well as that of the person you are helping. It involves a knowledge of the kinds of reaction that may arise, and the kind of sensitive self-discipline that is necessary to sort out these feelings, without experiencing guilt over having the feelings in the first place.

When you can distinguish your own feelings, and can tolerate and deal with them without impatience or excessive fantasy, you can also see other people as separate individuals. Here is a checklist of questions to help you recognise some of the signals:

- What is behind my above average interest in this person?
- What am I trying to get from this relationship that I would not like to admit to myself?
- Am I always ready to argue with this person ... or always ready to agree?
- Do I overreact to statements that they make?
- Is there a reason why either I or the other person is always late?
- Do I feel bored with them?
- Do I find myself wanting to end the relationship or to hold on to it even though it should end?

Personal understanding and development

> **The more self-aware a manager is, the better their decision making and management and facilitation of others.**

So what do you need to be aware of?

One of the most important methods for personal development is to learn from and deal with mistakes. As we have already said, to be an effective counsellor you have to know and understand yourself. The following ideas summarise things that are written in some textbooks, but that you only get to **know** in life itself. They are not laws or commandments, but frameworks for personal understanding and development.

Listen to the client

In normal circumstances, the client is not there to outwit or humiliate you. (Even when they seem to do nothing but this, they are going through a process which may have little to do with you as an individual.) They really do want to describe their situation to you. Many of the problems arise because the counsellor cannot, or does not, listen to what the client says.

They frequently tell you what you are missing, in a variety of ways. They may interrupt you and say, 'No, that's not what I mean at all,' or 'That's close to what I mean, but it isn't quite right'.

Sometimes they let you know by not saying anything. This is normal feedback from people who feel their message has not been received. If people feel their words will be misinterpreted, they have no reason to continue their story. Sometimes they try again, sometimes they just close up.

What are some of the signs that people are feeling unheard? Use of phrases like:

> 'Yes, but ...' (this means no ...)
> 'Well that might be so, but ...'

115

'Well, let me put it another way ...'

'No, it's not that ...'

Here is an example of a member of staff talking to his manager. He is saying that there is something wrong that he would like to correct.

Mr A: Well, I don't know what to make of it. I get up in the morning, I want to do my best, have a good day. Then I get down to breakfast and, before I know what is happening, I'm having a quarrel with my wife.

Manager: I suppose you're upset because you've been having trouble with your wife.

Mr A: No, it's not that. It's more that I don't seem to be able to avoid arguments. I'll be sitting in the coffee lounge and, for no reason at all, I react to something someone says and end up arguing over something trivial.

Mr A is trying to communicate his frustration with a seeming lack of self-control. While this could be seen as an example of not reflecting the question skilfully, the manager is also seizing on a specific example and responding directly to the incident, not the global feelings. In this case, the client helps the counsellor by changing the example.

So why did the manager miss the message?

This happens to veterans as well as novices. Sometimes the counsellor is listening to something else. Sometimes they have expectations of what the person might say, or what their problem is, and the assumption will take over. (Sometimes the problem may be too close to home for the counsellor.)

One way of checking whether you are hearing the client is if, at the end of the session, they are still trying to say the same thing they were saying at the beginning of the session.

> **Concentrate on the person, not the problem.**

There is a great danger of focusing on the problem, rather than the person who is experiencing it. **Problems do not exist in a vacuum**. There are only *people with problems*, and your response should be to the person.

If you concentrate too much on the problem, you run the risk of distorting the situation, or even looking at the wrong problem.

> **You do not have to solve the problem: you only have to help other people accept that responsibility for themselves.**

The problem can only be understood in the context of the person who experiences it. If you get the individual into the correct focus, you will automatically get the problem(s) into an accurate perspective.

The less a counsellor feels obliged to 'solve a problem', the more freely they can communicate the strength and support that the client needs, in order for them to find a solution.

It is a great relief for counsellors to realise that they do not have to solve every problem, or have an answer for every difficulty. Apart from allowing the counsellor to leave responsibility for the situation with the client, it is worth remembering that **very few 'problems' have 'solutions'**. There is very rarely a formula that a client can pick up, look at and say if I do that, then this will happen. Most of the time, the counsellor's role will be to help a client understand, accept and learn how to deal with their situation.

Success is not in your hands

It is common for bright people to want to 'do well'. There is nothing wrong per se with the desire to achieve. What has to be considered is how much that desire can interfere with helping others.

What are the elements of this need, or motivation?

Frequently, people who want to do well at all costs view others as opportunities for achievement, rather than as individuals. These people find it hard to look at life without the feeling that they must produce and earn gold stars, or else they will be deemed unworthy. They perceive 'value' as something that only someone else has the power to give them. They do not believe it to be inherent in themselves. Because of this lack of belief in themselves for what they are, they find it necessary to emulate an 'expert'. This makes it very hard for them to be natural or creative with a client. They are also so aware of the need to prove themselves, that it overrides their ability to see people objectively and as individuals. This need is not a conscious need, but it is important for the counsellor to know it exists.

118

> **The personality of the counsellor is their chief asset: you have to know the personality before using it to full effect.**

Don't rescue

Some people have a need to rearrange people's lives and provide them with happy endings. This raises several issues:

- Whose needs are being met – the counsellor's or the client's?
- What are you doing for others when you tell them what they should or should not do?

- What are you doing for yourself when you tell others what to do?
- Whose situation or problem is it when you take over?
- The need to take over is not confined to the new counsellor. Old hands frequently feel the need to 'take control'.

You do not help the client by taking over. In doing this, the problem becomes *yours* not theirs. If anything goes wrong with your solution, the blame will be transferred to you. Should everything go well, the client will not perceive it to be *their* achievement, and will not fully understand what has happened. It will therefore be very difficult for them to gain any insight into their own behaviour, or transfer any learning to a new situation. It may make the client more vulnerable or **dependent**. This means that the next time an issue arises they will come back to the counsellor to tell them what to do. They are relying on someone else to tell them what to do. This is not personal growth. The client may have an instant answer to their situation, but no understanding. It is important to question, not only the client's dependence on the counsellor, but also the counsellor's dependence on the client:

- Why do you feel the need to tell the client what to do?
- Does it make you feel stronger in yourself, being able to tell others what to do?
- Do you want to show them (and yourself) how much you know or how capable you are?
- Do you need to show them (and yourself) how powerful you are?
- Is there a subconscious attraction to the client?

All these thoughts, unpalatable as they may seem, are often around the counsellor's mind. They are perfectly reasonable in the light of our natural need to be approved of and liked. In the counselling situation they have to be controlled so that your

119

needs are of secondary importance to the client's. This increased self-awareness is an extremely important by-product of the counselling process for the counsellor. It has obvious implications for the manager in terms of self-development. They stand to gain almost as much as the client in those terms, but must always keep their needs in perspective.

One of the aims of helping others through counselling, is that the insights people gain will not only be useful in the specific situation but also in other situations. As a counsellor, it is important that you respect the client's potential to put into perspective what they are feeling, with your **guidance**, not your advice. Each individual has a different level of potential; some only need to verbalise a problem and they can see what they have to do; some take a fair amount of structured guidance. The counsellor has to assess this with each individual, while maintaining each time the basic tenet that it is the client's situation, not the counsellor's.

In management terms, this can sometimes seem difficult. If, for example, someone has a problem relating to work performance, it may not be possible, with time constraints, to 'let them be'. It is important to keep that as an ideal, but bear in mind that there is a grey area of 'suggestion' between giving advice and 'letting them be'.

It is crucial for the counsellor to understand why they react in a particular way towards a client. For example, on one occasion,

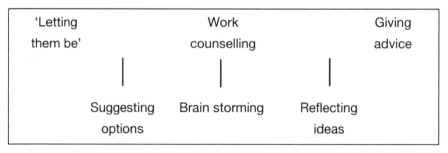

I watched someone trying to switch on a computer printer. They tried the switch twice, each time not quite turning it far enough. The third time they tried, they slammed their fist down on the printer, then turned the switch far enough. The printer sprang into action and they mumbled, 'The stupid thing only works when I hit it.'

Misunderstanding and/or misreading actions or reactions makes it hard to understand or deal with situations, as you are not working with accurate information. So it becomes easy for the counsellor to end up achieving 'solutions' without solving or even identifying the 'problem'.

So what do other people make us feel, that could damage the communication?

121

When you ask yourself the question, 'What is this person doing to me?', you begin to listen to the feelings that the person arouses in you. This is an important stage in both your development as a counsellor, and progressing your client. It puts the relationship in perspective, and protects you from inaccurate interpretation and inappropriate self-interest. You may be wondering how on earth you could get such complex dynamics when you have just called someone into your office to 'talk things through'. They will be there to a greater or lesser degree, depending on the relationship you have with the person, how skilled you are, the type of situation you are dealing with. Let's look at some examples of the reactions you may feel.

Feeling helpless

This is a feeling that there is nothing you can do, that you have missed something, or are lacking knowledge or training. These may be perfectly valid explanations for the feeling. There may also be times when you feel helpless, but can't quite work out where this feeling is coming from. This most commonly occurs with the person who is passive and dependent, and who acts out a helpless role with everyone. If people do not want to accept responsibility for themselves or their actions, they often, subconsciously, act in a helpless way. This can be infectious, and as a counsellor you are particularly vulnerable to this kind of behaviour, if you are under pressure from other commitments, or are not fully aware of your own emotional reactions. Recognising what is happening is the first step to dealing with it. In this case, understanding why you feel helpless makes you feel *less* helpless and more in control. It helps to underline exactly who is the helpless one.

Feeling angry

122

As with feeling helpless, there may be very practical reasons for feeling hostility towards a client, reasons that you can easily identify. However, there are times when you may be on the receiving end of a client's personality game. When you find frustration and irritation building up inside you for no apparent reason, you may be dealing with a person whose difficulty is 'passive aggression'.

> *When you find frustration and irritation building up inside you for no apparent reason, you may be dealing with a person whose difficulty is 'passive aggression'.*

This problem manifests itself in a style that communicates hostility in a seemingly non-assaultive and indirect way. The problem can be seen in the reactions of others, and of course in yourself, because what you experience is what everyone else is experiencing. The clients with this problem are usually unaware that there is anything wrong with their behaviour and may not understand why they have difficulties with relationships at work. Passive aggression is one of the most frequently reported reasons for counselling at work, and staff are referred by their bosses, usually because of problems about how they relate to others. They do not experience any anxiety and so are not very strongly motivated to change their behaviour. (They do not see it as a concern.) They will do things like turn up late for meetings, cancel at the last minute, or agree to something in principle, but not commit themselves. They seem to know how to be unco-operative at the moment when it will do the most harm. They hurt others, not by doing things, but by failing to do things. This thinking goes on at a psychological level of which they are not aware.

This is a very common situation and it is difficult not to be affected by this style of behaviour. It is important that you are aware that the anger you are experiencing may be coming from the client's 'camouflaged' behaviour. Unless you can understand that your anger is a response to the invisible 'passive aggression' of the client, you run the risk of expressing your hostility in a way that is inappropriate and may damage the relationship. Once you recognise the behaviour, you will feel more in control of your feelings and see the situation in a clearer perspective.

Feeling frightened

This may not happen as often as feeling angry, but is nevertheless something to be aware of. When you cannot find the source of your uneasiness, you may be dealing with a particularly complex personality which may demand a referral. The kind of person we are describing has the power to make people feel uneasy. This comes from the hostility that is buried just underneath the surface of what appears to be an 'intact' self-presentation. They may appear distant, but also quite impressive, especially on first association. This quickly wears thin, and as Mackinnon and Michels noted, 'As people know him better, they like him less'. They can change the atmosphere in a group, and can make others argumentative and resentful although they sometimes seem obsessed with fairness and 'being fair'. Although there is no one close to them, they can be acutely sensitive to the feelings of others. They generate a feeling of suspicion that keeps other people on their guard.

There are many reasons for this behaviour and, in this chapter, we are flagging it up as a potential issue for the counsellor to be aware of. This cannot be done unless you listen and understand yourself.

Feeling depressed

124

This is an issue which demands careful thought by the counsellor. It normally happens as a result of frustration or anger with a client, that you cannot express in the interview. Subconsciously, the anger gets turned in on yourself and you become depressed. Many clients will actually try to irritate or anger you; this is a way of them feeling more powerful than the person to whom they have come for help. Not only does it make them feel superior, but it also allows them to avoid dealing with their own issues. They seem to have an uncanny knack of working out exactly what will wind the counsellor up. Some of the things they say are subtle put-downs, designed to find the counsellor's Achilles' heel. For example, phrases like:

'I don't suppose you would be able to deal with that'
'That's not really your speciality, is it'
'Well, if that's what you think'
'I don't seem to be able to get my message across'

Part of you knows that it is not appropriate for you to get hostile with the client, so you repress the feeling and it frequently emerges as depression or discouragement.

The client's objective in this is not clear to them. They are also operating like this at a subconscious level. The client will only realise that this is what they are doing, and its implications, if the counsellor is aware of this process and can read behaviours accurately. They then need to explain it to the client.

When you cannot find reasons for your reactions, it is very easy to feel what the client is trying to make you feel, because it seems to be the only path on offer. This 'joining in' with the client is sometimes called **collusion**. Therefore an understanding of the processes is essential not only to avoid tension and stress in the counsellor, but also to enable the counsellor to feel they can deal with the situation itself.

The idea of the client turning all their complicated and unresolved problems onto the counsellor is called **projection**. It is also possible for an inexperienced counsellor, who is experiencing some problems of their own, to 'project' their problems on to the client.

125

Counselling tools

To summarise, the following are essential counselling tools:
It is reassuring for counsellors to understand that their feelings are not 'all their own fault', and that their confusion is not just a product of their inadequacy in the situation. Understanding

---

- **know yourself and your reactions**
- **listen to the client**
- **concentrate on the person, not the problem**
- **don't rescue**
- **respond to the person instead of trying to make a good response.**

your reactions allows you to see issues in perspective and to use your skills productively.

Being able to use your own reactions is a crucial part of the counselling process, and should be seen as a challenge to be mastered, rather than a barrier. Managers and counsellors who learn to listen to staff and clients through their own reactions will feel more confident, competent and able to perform more effectively.

9

Making a referral

Summary

Referring clients is an important issue for counsellors. This is particularly true for managers for whom counselling is only a part of their role. It is important that counsellors understand why they are referring a client. Once the decision to refer has been agreed and understood, it is part of the counsellor's role to be aware of the resources available, and how to contact them.

When referring a client, it is important for counsellors to:

- **understand their reasons for referral**
- **be prepared for the feelings they may experience when they refer**
- **understand the mechanics of referral**
- **be aware of local and national resources.**

Making a referral

Referring clients to other professionals is an important issue for counsellors. It is especially important for managers who counsel as part of their responsibilities, and who may frequently come across times when it may not be appropriate for them to act as counsellors. There are many situations in the counselling process where the counsellor may feel that the best thing for the client is to refer them on. The way you, as a counsellor, raise the issue of referral should allow your clients to explore the reasons for the suggestion. You should also ensure that the client feels it is their decision to decide whether or not to follow up the referral suggestion. (Deciding not to has implications for accepting the consequences of doing so.)

Referral may occur at several stages in the interview:

1 **When agreeing the initial contract:** It might happen that early on in the initial session, when you are setting the contract and discussing goals and outcomes, it becomes apparent on listening to the client's expectations that you are either not going to be able to deal with the issue, or it is not appropriate that you deal with it. At this point the counsellor might make a summary, ending with, 'Based on what you have been telling me, I'm wondering if you should consider seeing ... (then state the nature of the referral agency, for example, a careers guidance counsellor). If you wish to pursue this, I can probably recommend a suitable person.'

   It is also constructive to add your reasons, 'My reasons for suggesting this are ...'.

2 **At the end of the first session:** When you are referring back to your original contract at the end of the first session, you might summarise and say something along the lines of, 'We've talked about ... and it seems that, on the basis of what

you have said, it might be helpful for you to consider seeing ... (referral agency)', and then explain your reasons.

3 **When the relationship has been established:** Whilst the mechanics of doing the referring at this stage are similar to the other two stages, this stage is more complex as the relationship has been established and may be changed by referral.

This leads on to exploring the feelings that counsellors have, both when making referrals and, in some cases, for not making them.

Feelings of counsellor when referring

Abandoning the person

Some counsellors feel guilty about handing over their clients to someone else. Referral stirs up many feelings about this, particularly in those counsellors who are very hard on themselves, who feel they cannot make a mistake, even the kind that veteran counsellors make. A good referral is not abandoning the individual, but is a recommendation in the individual's best interest.

Getting rid of the person

Referral can easily represent more of a solution for the counsellor than the client, for example, they may have become resentful that the client ever knocked on the office door in the first place, and just want to be rid of them. This is not true in most of the cases that are successfully referred.

Feeling you have failed

Referring a client may generate in you a feeling that you are not good enough, or you have failed, or are letting down the client in some way.

Unless you deal with your feelings about the client before referral, you may give the impression of rejecting the individual with whom you are working. This does not mean you should be hesitant about the referral, this will only make the client feel the same way. This could leave the relationship of the counsellor and the client unsettled and ambiguous. You should not be afraid of letting the client express positive or negative feelings towards you, and should attempt to explore and clarify them. It is important to handle these feelings and not to take them too personally: they are an essential part of the counselling process. People who have a need for close contact with others will find it difficult to deal with these issues, as they feel it may make people dislike them. It is back to your motivation for counselling and back to the questions 'Who is the counselling for? What is in the best interest of the client?'.

Referral should not be seen as a 'cut-off', but rather as a logical outcome of the process the counsellor and client have gone through. Ideally, it should not be a total surprise to the client; it should be perceived by both counsellor and client as a possibility from the outset.

This includes telling the truth to the client about the reasons for referral. However embarrassed or bad you feel, it is not appropriate to disguise the reason for the referral. Fabricated reasons never ring true, and a simple statement from the counsellor about why they are making the referral takes very little time and is an expression of an honest relationship. This has particularly serious implications for a manager who has been counselling someone who they see regularly in the course of work.

130

What might be the reasons for referral?

These are some of the main reasons for referral:

- the counsellor might feel that the needs of the client are beyond their capabilities at that time
- the counsellor feels that the client needs help on a long-term basis, which they may not have time for, nor may it be appropriate for them to do so
- the relationship does not seem to be working, despite repeated efforts
- there may be a personality mismatch between counsellor and client
- the line management relationship is in conflict with the counselling relationship.

The fundamental principle of referral is that it is always in the greater interest of the individual. The question you have to ask yourself is 'What is the best thing for the client at this time?'.

You should be willing to answer questions about the referral and explore the client's feelings about it so that clear boundaries are established even though you may be about to end the relationship.

The process of referral ends with the counsellor moving out of the picture, with the establishment of another professional's responsibility for the client. In terms of the manager's role, it is important that they are seen to support the client in the workplace, although the counselling relationship has terminated.

Counsellors should have a collection of names, addresses and telephone numbers of referral agencies available to them. It is helpful to build up a network of different people with different skills. Internally, these should include people like the company doctor and named individuals in the personnel and training departments. There is a list of the major agencies at the back of the book, but it is helpful to compile a local list for yourself. No list is exhaustive and it is also helpful to establish contacts with caring professionals

The counsellor who knows whom to call at the right moment, is well equipped for referrals.

in the community who might be able to advise you of other referral agencies. For example, Alcoholics Anonymous can be very helpful in dealing with some of the problems you come up against. A contact at local agencies can relieve a great deal of personal stress from the counsellor. The counsellor who knows whom to call at the right moment, is well equipped for referrals.

132

There is a baffling array of counselling and psychological services available and it is sometimes difficult for the manager, as counsellor, to distinguish between them. There is not really a way of legislating for each problem either, so we cannot say, 'If … happens, you should …', because each individual is different. The organisations mentioned in Appendix IV should discuss with you the particular situation and help you assess whether they can provide the appropriate help.

Stressful occasions are those in which environmental or internal demands (or both) tax or exceed the adaptive resources of an individual

LAZARUS AND LAUNIER

10

Cause and effect in a changing environment

Summary

In this chapter we examine a very important aspect of management, namely how to deal with stress in organisations which are undergoing a rapid process of change.

While different individuals find different things stressful and respond differently to stressful situations, there are a number of common physical and psychological symptoms associated with stress. We look in particular at the way 'burn out' can lead to feelings of futility andpersonal failure.

Almost any kind of change – good or bad – is stressful to some degree. We examine the major sources of stress at work, many of which are exacerbated by periods of radical organisational change. The responsibility for managing other people makes managers' jobs particularly stressful. We look at some of the pressures on managers, from dealing with the stresses affecting their own staff, to the all-too-common problem of overwork.

Both organisations and individuals can minimise the stresses associated with organisational change. We argue that both organisations and individuals need first, to recognise the signs of stress and secondly, to face up to the problem. We look at ways of measuring the stress levels of organisations and ways in which managers can set about tackling stress among their staff. We argue that employee counselling, far from being a

135

luxury, is a necessity of enlightened business practice.

Finally, we look at how individuals – both managers and workers alike – can tackle their own stress levels. More important than the choice of methods of relaxation is to develop a sense of perspective. This can be achieved by using counselling to enable individuals to develop a scheme of personal values which can help to determine their actions and evaluate their own circumstances.

Stress

Stress – both individual and organisational – is one of the most obvious results of the kind of radical organisational and environmental change which forms much of the subject-matter of this book. One of the most important techniques that innovative managers in changing organisations need to learn is how to deal with this stress.

A great deal of attention has been paid to the new circumstances facing organisations, and the way in which the changing demographic, technological and sociological features of the business environment have affected the way they operate. But rather less attention has been paid to the impact of these changes on *individuals* in organisations. We have some idea of what we should be doing about training and retraining. Companies have accepted some responsibility for easing the pains of redundancy, but we have paid less attention to the stresses and strains which these changes are imposing on those remaining in employment.

Recognising stress

Modern life, and modern management in particular, is beset by stressful events, from production deadlines to managing a meeting in a foreign language, or pulling together a team which seems intent on pulling itself apart.

However, the point at which our normal coping mechanisms cease to be effective on these occasions and when we start to suffer from stress differs for each one of us. At one end of the scale are the highly nervous, anxious types who have difficulty in coping even with a quiet domestic life and may not be capable of holding down any sort of a job. At the other end are the people capable of handling world-wide responsibilities, or stepping into a capsule to be fired off into outer space. However, whatever our own personal capacity for adjustment, once that capacity is over-stretched, each of us begins to suffer the mental and physical symptoms of stress.

137

The lifestyles of the Western world ensure that certain periods of life are stressful for most of us. Our early years are taken up with learning ways of relating to others which will powerfully affect our future. It is also likely that we will face particular challenges in adolescence and mid-life, and on retirement.

It is when life's daily challenges become excessive that stress begins to manifest itself. One of the most revealing symptoms of stress is a distorted sense of time, often caused by the desire to do things faster. Some doctors and counsellors diagnose stress by asking an individual to sit in a chair and say when they think a minute has elapsed. One doctor recalled a manager who thought a minute had elapsed after just nine seconds!

One of the most revealing symptoms of stress is a distorted sense of time, often caused by the desire to do things faster.

Stress becomes apparent through both physical and psychological symptoms. It can manifest itself in feelings of dissatisfaction and a continuing feeling of being overburdened, as well as by physiological measures such as blood pressure, cholesterol levels, heart rate and adrenaline excretion. It is also apparent in the incidence of ulcers, heart attacks and other stress-related illnesses, and by changes in health-related behaviour such as smoking and drinking.

One doctor recalled a manager who thought a minute had elapsed after just nine seconds!

Stress can, in fact, contribute to or trigger off a whole host of physical illnesses: high blood pressure, heart disease, chronic backache, bronchial asthma, dermatitis and eczema, diabetes, migraines, peptic ulcers and alcohol or drug dependence. Moreover, people under stress often adopt health-damaging behaviours such as reducing sleep, smoking and drinking excessively and eating poorly-balanced diets.

Long before illness is established, however, individuals under stress will experience psychological reactions. They may become aware of increased irritability with others, or else become indecisive if too many important matters suddenly have to be decided in a hurry. Under prolonged strain, individuals may begin to wonder if anything is worthwhile. Boredom and depression increase and so does a general dislike of other people. Social skills deteriorate, responses become clumsier and more offensive, the will to communicate with anyone at all is weakened.

A sense of stress easily translates into a feeling of being persecuted and unable to cope. An individual may suffer feelings of futility and failure and lose their sense of personal worth. 'Burn out', sometimes called the disease of modern life, is a particular form of stress, typified by emotional exhaustion and the inabil-

138

ity to respond to others as human beings or to carry out work of a normal standard.

Burn out has three main dimensions:

- physical and mental exhaustion, a loss of feeling and concern, and a loss of interest and spirit
- negative or inappropriate reactions to other people, loss of idealism and irritability
- negative perceptions of oneself, low morale, depression and reduced productivity or capability.

Most of all, someone with burn out experiences personal dissatisfaction and a sense of failure in relation to the goals that are important to him or her.

139

The stresses of change

Almost any kind of change, 'good' or 'bad', creates stress. One scale of 'stress value', developed by Holmes and Rahe,[1] ranks marriage as the seventh most stressful of the 43 'life happenings'. Marital reconciliation comes ninth, pregnancy twelfth, and outstanding personal achievement around mid-way on the list.

Holmes and Rahe also looked at the stress caused by changes at work. On a scale of 1 to 100, on which the death of a spouse scores 100, they gave the following scores to work and work-related changes:

Business readjustments	39
Change to a different line of work	36
Change in responsibilities at work	29
Change in living conditions	25
Change in work hours or conditions	20
Change in residence	20
Change in social activities	18

Some well-defined sources of stress at work are:

- working conditions
- poor job definitions
- relationships
- changing roles
- responsibility for other people
- value conflicts.

Each of these potential sources of stress can become more pronounced in times of organisational change.

Some kinds of work appear to be particularly stressful for some types of people, while some kinds of work appear to be stressful to many people. Stress can be minimised by careful matching of the needs of the worker to the requirements of the job. How well-suited an individual is to a particular job is more than a matter of resilience to stress, of course. It involves all aspects of his or her temperament, ability and motivation. For instance, people who perform best when they are guided by rules, receive strong leadership and know exactly what they have to do, will suffer particularly badly if put into ambiguous or fluctuating conditions. Also, great stress can be caused to individuals who are given a job which requires them to work much faster or slower than their 'natural' pace.

A job which superficially seems to suit an individual well may still contain elements which they cannot master and which are therefore major sources of stress. Those high on logic but low on creativity, for instance, can impose great burdens upon themselves and others if they are put into a job where new solutions are regularly required.

Particularly stressful change is characterised by:

- being unpredictable and unfamiliar
- being involuntarily imposed

- demanding a high *degree* of change
- demanding *very rapid* change
- denying individuals any feedback on whether their attempts to cope with events are succeeding
- denying individuals the warmth and support of their colleagues.

There is potential for much misunderstanding, waste of effort, sense of unfairness and general anxiety when members of staff are left uncertain about their work objectives and responsibilities as a result of major organisational change. There may be differences with bosses and with colleagues over the tasks to be done, and disagreement about the extent of responsibility to be exercised in carrying out a task effectively. Interference from above may seem excessive; on the other hand, a superior's support may seem quite inadequate.

141

Discrepancies between employees' responsibility and their authority, as a result of restructuring, can seriously reduce their capacity to carry out the job. Again, in a restructured team where the manager is not on site and lines of responsibility and authority are not clearly defined, the manager may be subject to conflicting loyalties to the home office and to the team, which will have an adverse effect on the team's performance.

In times of change, if structures are not provided to help employees cope with new ways of working, and people start to feel unsafe, stress takes over. Whatever their level of resilience, everyone shares the need for equilibrium, to make sense of their experiences and the events around them and to feel that they have some degree of control over them. If this equilibrium becomes damaged, people will start to feel stressed.

The stresses of management

One of the most important sources of stress, as we have seen, is responsibility for other people. The jobs that have been found to carry the highest levels of stress – miners, policemen, construction workers, doctors, dentists and managers – all involve a high degree of responsibility for the safety and well-being of others.

As well as coping with the stress of their staff, managers working in organisations that are undergoing major change will also face undoubted stres-

The jobs that have been found to carry the highest levels of stress ...

142 ses in their own role. They have to sustain relationships, to cope with pressures from above and below and from outside the organisation, to deal with friction, accept blame for subordinates' limitations, confront outsiders on behalf of the department, confront subordinates where necessary, and attend often demanding and seemingly unproductive meetings.

Conventional wisdom paints a picture of the nineties as being less obsessed with careers than the previous decade. Nevertheless, many managers are still struggling with overwork. Those who have survived downsizing and restructuring are often so concerned about keeping their place in the organisation that they feel pressure to be seen to be doing more. Many companies change their working practices and structures without thinking about how to reshape the resulting workload.

Because every individual reacts differently, it is hard to generalise about what overwork really is. One manager's exhilarating schedule is another's impossible grind. In Japan, the phenomenon of *karoshi*, death by overwork, usually means death from a heart attack. But this phenomenon may not generally be caused so much by long working hours, as by the mental attitude of Japanese workers. It is certainly not confined to Japan.

However, while there are some managers who may thrive on a 13-hour day, most people do not. The ones who do are usually those who love what they are doing and are fulfilled by their work. The health risks of hating your job have been known to medical researchers in the US since 1972, when a Massachusetts study showed that dissatisfaction with your job was a strong predictor of heart disease. Over the past 20 years, many other research projects have confirmed this finding.

... all involve a high degree of responsibility for the safety and well-being of others.

143

However, many medical practitioners, while happy to say 'eat more healthily' or 'give up smoking', would be very unwilling to say 'leave your job'. Of course, leaving the job is not the only alternative. It may be just as helpful for an individual to accept his or her situation and put work in perspective.

It is important to remember that longer hours do not necessarily result in higher productivity, but frequently have the opposite effect, as people become too tired to think clearly and act effectively. Of course, it is difficult to prove that a company would make better decisions and be more innovative if their managers were less busy and less tired. However, there is undoubtedly a danger that successful, senior people in an organisation reach the point where they can only feel they are doing their job properly if they are running on water. Very soon, this idea filters through the organisation until it affects all the workers.

In one British organisation undergoing a major restructuring exercise, managers were badly prepared to deal with the inevitable conflicts and demands arising from the new emphasis on devolution of responsibility. Caught in the middle, between the executives who wanted to push change through and the workers given the job of implementing it, the managers tried to please everybody. Their way of 'coping' was to formulate vague and often ambiguous objectives.

Because the managers in this organisation had very little sense of control, they increasingly relied on bureaucratic mechanisms to get things done, creating more paperwork. Some of their staff became increasingly resistant to change and the pressure on the managers intensified. Many could not cope and 'burnt out', thus putting even more pressure on their staff.

In stressful situations, managers are often their own worst enemies. Henry Mintzberg, the American writer and professor, comments that the pressures of many managers' jobs drive them to be superficial in their actions. He suggests that they tend to overload themselves with work, encourage interruption, respond quickly to every stimulus, seek the tangible and avoid the abstract, make decisions in small increments, and do everything abruptly. As well as increasing the stress on themselves, these tendencies reduce managers' efficiency at work.

Dealing with stress in an organisation

As we have seen, organisational change is a potential source of major stress for workers and managers alike. Let us now examine the steps managers and their organisations can take to minimise the harmful effects of stress.

The first thing to be done, of course, is to recognise the signs of stress in an organisation. Although individuals are likely to be the first to experience the mental or physical signs of stress, these private warnings are likely, sooner or later, to be translated into behaviours which others can observe. For instance, a good timekeeper might start coming in late; someone who always meets deadlines begins to miss them; or a constructive member of a team might become an irritable nit-picker who makes untypical attacks on others.

Some of the following groups of behaviour should also signal to a manager that a member of staff is suffering from stress:

- The individual is eager to please, wants to help rather than to take responsibility, is looking for a friend, cannot accept success, constantly worries about failure, is dependent on others, is indecisive, is always taking on new work, never completes to deadlines, is constantly at meetings.
- The individual is aggressive, talks 'at' you, doesn't listen, bosses others, is obstinate, has fixed views and opinions, is autocratic, unwilling to delegate, critical, and contemptuous of others, is unreasoned and envious, and cannot take criticism.
- The individual cannot organise his or her own work properly, blames others constantly, finds it difficult to finish jobs, is defensive and secretive, has few friends, is irrational and prone to panic, avoids personal contact, is unco-operative and sometimes deprecating about the organisation, uses memos too often, puts off work, is anxious.

145

Behaviour at meetings is also a very useful indicator of stress in an organisation. In a 'healthy' meeting, everyone contributes, problems are shared and members show a recognition of each other's values and a determination to resolve difficulties together. Meetings of people who are under stress are markedly different. Discussion will tend to be aggressive, and some members will attack while others withdraw into passivity. There is much searching for scapegoats, and plenty of non-verbal behaviour indicating withdrawal, lack of interest and hostility. The behaviour of key players in any team is crucial. Once they demonstrate disaffection, poor morale will quickly spread through the whole group.

An organisation concerned about levels of stress among its employees may choose to design its own survey. For example, a simple questionnaire might list work elements which are known to be a source of stress, such as work overload, time pressures and deadlines, travel, poor consultation, attending meetings, office politics, and so on, and ask staff to tick the five they find most stressful. A section for any additional sources of stress experienced can provide useful additional information.

146

Once the signs of stress have been recognised, managers need to face up to the problems this poses the organisation. During a period of radical organisational change, it is very important that managers should be able to help their staff to cope with the stress they may experience. The process of adjustment required is too often damaged by a manager's evasions and platitudes ('You'll soon get over it'), or by putting off discussion ('I'll see you about it next week'). Some managers escape from the need to address the issue by pulling rank ('Sorry, but I really am pressed. The show must go on. Personnel will see you.') Others offer palliatives which may or may not alleviate but which amount to evasion ('Take the afternoon off').

Ignoring or evading the signs of stress runs the danger of lowered productivity and poor team morale, as well as damage to the well-being of individuals.

Ignoring or evading the signs of stress runs the danger of lowered productivity and poor team morale, as well as damage to the well-being of individuals. Enlightened self-interest, at least, requires that organisations undergoing major change or other stressful experiences should investigate ways of relieving the strains these can cause.

Among the measures organisations could consider, employee counselling must surely come high on the list. Whether or not the wider circumstances of the organisation can be changed, counselling can help individuals to make constructive moves to ease their own situation, or at least to accept what must be accepted. It can speed the process of coming to terms with change, and check the development of damaging reactions which rebound upon other staff. For many organisations in the current climate of change, counselling is not a luxury service, nor even an integral part of a humane personnel programme, but simply sound business practice.

147

Managers need to be able to recognise patterns of stressed behaviour in their staff which can be dealt with by counselling. Counselling can perhaps offer the greatest benefits as a preventative measure, when the early signs of stress have been recognised, or even before. Although it is not possible to predict people's behaviour with certainty, there are some situations which will create stress for most people, most of the time. At times of change, in particular, managers should consider introducing counselling programmes well before any overt signs of stress have become apparent.

Dealing with stress as an individual

Organisations can act to minimise the effects of stress. But, of course, there are a number of ways in which individuals can reduce their own stress levels.

As with organisations, the first step for any individual is to recognise that he or she is suffering from stress. There is a strong temptation either to deny that it exists or to give up altogether and go under. However, the effective management of stress involves, first, an awareness of the stress experienced by yourself and others and, secondly, an awareness of the options available to reduce it. Without an awareness of your own experience of stress, you are very unlikely to find an appropriate remedy.

A positive approach to managing stress very often involves deciding what is important in your life and measuring everything else against those values.

Sometimes very traumatic experiences, such as the early death of a friend, or a child's sickness, lead people to put their lives in perspective. For one manager, this was exactly what happened (see the example below).

148

Case study

John had been working extremely hard, immersed in what he was doing, to the extent that he was unable to see what his work priorities were, let alone his personal values. His company was pushing all its employees very hard, but his reaction, like many others in the company, had simply been to work harder and harder. He became irritable with his family and colleagues, shouted at his secretary, and missed deadlines.

However, at this point his youngest child was found to have a potentially life threatening disease. The manager dropped everything at work, spent three days at his son's hospital bed, and then returned to work to await further medical tests. He arrived at his desk, looked at the mounds of paper which had accumulated over three days, and suddenly realised that the paper 'did not amount to a hill of beans' in comparison to the health of his son. It was as if someone had opened a window for him.

With a wider perspective, and able to see the wood for the trees, he was able to get through his mound of paper in no time. He felt calmer and more able to cope. When the medical tests gave his son a clean bill of health, he did not lose his new-found perspective, and has felt himself to be far more efficient as a result.

There are a wide range of different ways of reducing stress. It doesn't matter whether you decide to meditate once a day, or diet, or work out twice a week. Recharging the batteries can take many forms depending on individual taste, including walking, watching films, playing with your children, or bungee jumping!

Whatever form of relaxation you decide to adopt, the really important thing is to decide what things make life worth living for you. It could be always leaving work on time, never taking work home, reading, watching football or climbing mountains. Actually doing these things should be the physical manifestation of a deeper, internal decision to put life into perspective.

149

For some people, there comes a point when they realise that they are working 70 hours a week and they don't know why. These people, who are unlikely to have given much previous thought to their life priorities, may finally decide they have to get off the overwork treadmill, take better care of themselves, and give more time to their personal life. The interesting thing is that those who do decide what is important to them, and take action accordingly, are often able to work more productively. It is in these circumstances that the manager has a key role as a counsellor, to enable their colleagues to come to the decisions that will enhance both their individual performance and their contribution to the organisation.

People with a clear sense of their own priorities are generally also better able to cope with change. Not only are they likely to be more successful as individuals, but their employer is more likely to benefit from their motivation and from the improved morale of the people around them. Their internal 'stability' will often have a knock-on effect on the people they work with, making them calmer too. Stressed managers tend to produce stressed teams or departments, but the reverse is also true: self-aware, calm and focused managers can produce a healthy department, able to respond positively and innovatively to change.

Reference

[1] Holmes, T. H. and Rahe, R.H., *Rahe's Social Readjustment Scale*, Journal of Psychosomatic Research, Vol. 11, 1967

11

Developing a facilitating environment for change

Summary

In most organisations, the major casualty in times of change is communication. Yet sensitive communication is the factor which can make the difference between rapid adaptation with an enthusiastic workforce and general disenchantment.

Good personnel policies and practices help. They are complemented by planned, comprehensive programmes of communication. These should include: well-publicised commitment to staff well-being; objective assessment of employee attitudes; special programmes of communication developed in relation to any major change. Introducing equal opportunity and making relocation easier are two major changes which benefit from such planning. Employees can also be encouraged and helped to take care of their own mental and physical health. A counselling service can complement and reinforce the value of all these measures. It needs careful, systematic introduction.

The counselling role during times of change

In times of change, great vigour is required to push through restructuring, introduce new technology and implement new policies and ideas which the situation demands. The lesson has now been learned, sometimes the hard way, that as much energy needs to be put into care and concern for staff as is put into the mechanics of change, if expected benefits are to be realised.

Even when no major change is occurring, divisions and units may be experiencing stressful times and individuals undergoing stress in ways and to a degree by no means always appreciated by top management.

Many potential difficulties in achieving dynamic change without damaging people can be offset by good personnel management policies and practices. As an example, careful selection, placement and promotion can do much to avert the strains resulting both from inappropriate appointments and also from vague job descriptions of tasks and responsibilities. Job descriptions which are accurate enough to provide a basis for a person specification will also serve to reduce role ambiguities and the conflicts they can provoke. Skilful induction

Marks and Spencer reduced wastage of trainees on their graduate training schemes by the simple process of seeking selection interviewers' advice as to the type of store which would best suit each candidate.

can do much to ensure that newcomers become as happy and useful as possible in the shortest possible time, as well as reducing wastage. Marks and Spencer reduced wastage of trainees on their graduate training schemes by the simple process of seeking selection interviewers' advice as to the type of store which would best suit each candidate. The initially shy benefited from a time in a small quiet store whilst the over-confident discovered the size of their task in stores in central London.

Promotion also demands careful matching. It is no longer a question of rewarding those who have shown most diligence or served the longest. Such a policy today can simply result in turning a highly competent and satisfied computer programmer into an ineffective and unhappy systems analyst or a first class salesman into a poor sales manager with consequent distress for everyone in the team. The person with appropriate abilities must be put in the post and alternative ways of recognising and rewarding achievements and high performance found for the programmer and salesman.

But something additional to good personnel practices is required if morale is to be sustained in conjunction with flexibility and rapid adaptation to change. What is needed is a very high level of communication and of sensitivity in everyday management. This chapter reviews some practices which may help an organisation to develop this standard of communication and, in particular, to introduce an effective counselling service.

Issue a mission statement

A company determined to maintain creative levels of change, whilst reducing its adverse impacts, might begin by making a commitment to that effect. Commitments to avoid involuntary redundancy now frequently accompany statements about closures and mergers. A commitment to reduce other adverse effects of change as far as possible would go further. It would mean an acceptance that the company sees no value in stress, that the two-ulcer man has no place in its hall of fame and that it sees no merit in executives working overtime and at weekends. It would indicate that, in accepting responsibility for introducing change, the firm equally accepted responsibility for mitigating any of its effects.

Take the attitudinal temperature

It is dangerous to report bad news to one's superiors. Greek messengers bearing news of a defeat in battle were liable to have their heads cut off. Although company messengers receive less drastic treatment, it is hard for bosses to welcome anyone who has nothing but trouble to report, especially when they themselves are under pressure or when they themselves are the subject of criticism.

154

One large organisation decided for good reason to relocate several scattered units in one large office building. The pressures of moving on time led top management to skimp on explanations and consultation. Failure to explain why the move was decided upon, how the different groups would benefit and on what terms people would be employed in the new premises, led to widespread dissatisfaction. Managers' early warning reports were ignored or subject to the view that, 'everyone would settle down soon'. But long before anyone settled down, absenteeism and sickness rose and 50 per cent of key staff found other jobs. It was a classic case of the message being underplayed by overworked senior management, too preoccupied with the mechanics of change and their own situations to give due attention to the storm signals.

To gather objective information about staff attitudes, companies can commission attitude surveys. An independent consultant can conduct structured interviews with a stratified sample of staff and report on prevailing attitudes regarding a range of issues.

Questionnaires may also be used to yield objective and anonymous evidence of attitudes at different levels.

H & A Associates produced an Organisational Effectiveness Questionnaire by which individual's subjective experience of working in an organisation are translated into a general perception of factors such as: degree of formal control; amount of initiative permitted; the extent to which good work is recognised; the ease with which communication flows; the quality of contact between individuals; the sense of belonging to a supportive team; the clarity of goals for the organisation and the unit and the expectations regarding work standards. This can be used to benchmark and compare organisational performance over a period of time.

155

An organisation can also make use of subordinate surveys. Such surveys might require a subordinate to rate his/her boss in terms of ability to give a clear direction, to supply useful information, to enhance team spirit, to listen and encourage and so forth. A number of ratings by different subordinates are required to ensure anonymity of the individual rater. Scores are amalgamated (by an independent scorer) and the manager given the group result. Subordinate surveys are useful in management training, may indicate areas of potential stress and can help in appraisal.

Plan for minimal stress when implementing changes

In fulfilment of a mission statement, there are a number of steps which every concern can take to maintain morale and commitment whatever changes come to be required:

1 Give plans to reduce impact of change on the staff the same priority as is given to financial plans.

2 Regularly forecast possible sources of stress and plan to mitigate them.

3 Encourage a culture in which individuals accept responsibility for their own mental and physical health and are helped to maintain it.

4 Plan to tackle particular morale problems as they arise, for example:
   - the relocation of staff, particularly if going overseas.

5 Introduce, promote and support a counselling service available to all staff.

When introducing major change

The most important contribution to staff morale is likely to be a thorough and well planned programme of communication, designed to ensure that everyone receives written and spoken explanations of the change, why and when it is occurring and how they will be affected. The programme needs to be timetabled and planned to release accurate information ahead of the grapevine. Especial care must be taken to include those at junior levels in the organisation where the impact of change is least often explained. Managers must have the information to enable them to brief their departments and answer individual queries.

Information clinics, run by senior and respected people, can do much to supplement normal channels of communication or to allay any worries which have developed. When morale dropped in Ford Finance UK, the chief executive decided to conduct a canteen clinic once a month. For an hour during the lunch break he visited the canteen, with a promise to answer truthfully whatever questions were put to him. The hostility and fear revealed by the questions at early meetings gradually gave way to greater acceptance and a more constructive approach.

Taking the human factor into account from the outset must also involve retraining plans. A problem encountered by many firms on the introduction of computers has been the long delay between the arrival of the equipment and any realisation of its full potential. Too often it has been assumed that once the new machines are in, all systems will be simplified, all controls perfected and much needed information will

When morale dropped in Ford Finance UK, the chief executive decided to conduct a canteen clinic once a month. For an hour during the lunch break he visited the canteen, with a promise to answer truthfully whatever questions were put to him.

157

instantly be available. In practice, very few benefits are realised until all the staff, from the managers downwards, understand the equipment's possibilities and are, to some extent, competent in operating it. Retraining staff not only ensures that the equipment is properly used as quickly as possible but also reaffirms the value put upon staff retention.

Since major change gives rise to great feelings of insecurity it is important for the organisation to provide as much security as possible in policies and practices unaffected by change. Hygiene factors such as canteen services and living conditions need to be specially protected. The changes which British industry has seen over the past decade would have been even more traumatic without redundancy pay or redundancy counselling.

Companies will only be able to steer their way through the 'whitewater' of change if they not only have the plans for changes, but also ensure that managers have both the inter-personal skills and the opportunities to facilitate that change.

Appendices

∎

Appendix 1

■

Case Study One: Annotated counselling session transcript

These are transcripts of real interviews that took place between manager and individual, with the names changed. They are excerpts that are taken from different stages of the counselling process. The purpose is to illustrate some of the dynamics and techniques of the counselling session.

Session One: Margaret tries to set boundaries and keep David to them

Margaret   OK, David, you asked if we could have some time together, so perhaps you would like to start by telling me what it is you want to talk about.

Counsellor is trying to set boundaries for the conversation, and is stressing who initiated it

David   Well, I've been on holiday and I have a member of staff who I have talked to before about their performance. It seemed to get a lot better, but was a little like a roller coaster. Now we're back down at the bottom and I'm just finding it really hard work to keep on going in and saying, 'look, something is obviously the matter'. I'm really thinking that the issue this time is the same as last time. It is to do with their situation at home which has a really detrimental effect on the way they perform at work. I am really trying to think of and find ways in which I've … I guess really that I don't have to keep on picking them up off the bottom. If you imagine a big roller coaster going down the dip, I seem to find that at the bottom of the dip, you say, 'look, you need to get back on and up' and I find that quite difficult to keep on giving them that support. I really need some ideas on how I can help them keep on a more even keel. So, that is what I want to talk to you about because I really feel I've exhausted all the resources I have and I can get them back off the floor but it leaves me feeling frustrated and worn out and also thinking, well, you know, pull yourself together. However, on the other hand, I know that they have got major personal problems at home.

Margaret That sounds like there were two things you wanted to discuss; one of them is the problem itself, the issue that this person has and the other one is how you manage that person and all the issues that that presents.

David Well, I feel comfortable to sort out their problem, but I feel very uncomfortable about the way I manage them. They effectively help to keep me at a distance from managing them. I feel as though I never get to the bottom of the problem, and end up making suggestions which they either never take up, or they say don't work. I ask myself whether I have got the problem right in the first place, or whether I am just saying things they want to hear. I know they have very difficult personal problems, or rather, I think I know, but I don't know how to help them. I then end up being really irritated thinking that he is

Counsellor is trying to clarify client's confused thoughts, and trying to focus them on what they perceive to be the issue

time consuming and really needs to recognise that he needs to help himself.

Margaret That is moving back into the problem itself again, but perhaps first of all, we should establish what we can deal with now because what you have done is you've booked 20 minutes and it sounds like there is probably a longer issue than 20 minutes of time and, therefore, what we need perhaps to do within the 20 minutes is just frame out what the problem is. I suspect that we will have to put in some more time to deal with the issues that are facing you in managing the problem. I am not sure whether they can be separated, from what you have just said, from the issue itself because it sounds like they are pretty well entwined. However, I think that what we should do today is just establish exactly what the issues are and a framework for some more meetings where we can discuss it further.

Counsellor is setting boundaries for the session

David Well, it would help if I just outline where I think I got to and what the key things are that I have indicated, well, OK, I need some help.

Margaret That is a good idea, so let us see what the issue looks like.

David Right. Well, the person in question is currently going through a fairly acrimonious separation, or it is potentially acrimonious. They have separated from their partner through mental illness, on her behalf. The current issue is that they are extremely concerned about whether they will keep their job and will be able to

163

pay the increased amount of mortgage that they have been paying over the past nine months since the separation. They are also worried about the long-term implications that they may be called upon to pay medical bills, ad infinitum.

Margaret Can I just check something out – I am sorry to interrupt you at this point, but what you are describing are the current personal issues of this person. Have I got that right?

Counsellor is reminding client of boundaries

David Yes.

Margaret And I am wondering whether we should discuss that bit further or perhaps the bigger context of how you came to be dealing with the person in the first place.

David It was the context of that personal issue that has been following through, because it is always the same thing that we get to as the backdrop to their poor performance. I mean, this time I went in and said, 'look, why don't you tell me what is going on, because there is obviously something' and what triggered that off was I was having to pick up their work because it wasn't being done properly. The thing that I noticed this time was that, when I came back from holiday, he was demanding services from the rest of the team, which they found unreasonable. They were saying 'well, look, hang on, you are not treating us fairly'. I asked him what was going on, and to be brought up to speed to be told, 'oh well, they just need to sort themselves out'. Now, having heard the other side of the story, I suggested that perhaps at this point he ought to lend more support to the other members of the team. They had decided to put on a special dinner for him where they could clarify in everybody's mind exactly what was happening so that they could get on with their jobs.

What really concerned me was to get a comment like, 'well, it's not my job and they should be able to sort themselves out'. I pointed out that as a manager that was his job, and that I expected him to lend support to them even if it did mean like he was wiping their noses for them because that was what they needed from him at that time. His response to me was fairly curt, so I made it quite clear that that was what I expected. What I felt was 'well, you should be able to see that; you are a middle manager, you should see that that is what is required from you. I shouldn't have to point those sort of things out'. In addition, other work which I had asked for on more than one occasion, had not been completed. I had extended some deadlines for him because there were specific things that hadn't happened and then said, 'well, look, since I've been back from holiday, this has blown up, you haven't finished the work that you promised, and I need to see it first thing tomorrow morning.'

I was angry because I was having to follow those things up and realised that something was wrong by the look on his face and the fact that he looked terrible. So I said, 'look, there is obviously something

165

Client is already clearly expressing anger with their member of staff

going on, why don't you just tell me what is going on, so that I can try and help'. So that was how we came once again to this – I mean, I can describe it as sort of a boil bursting – that we get to the stage where I say, 'look, are we here again, what's the issue?'. When I talk to the person, it is because in their personal life the state that they are in has got to a point where it does roll over very much into their work, so it was the personal changes that he was going through, that had had such a drastic effect on his performance.

Margaret   So the reason you were explaining it to me, was because it is the 'crunch' point for this person; that is, their personal life at home is impacting on their work and that is when you pick it up as a manager.

Counsellor summarises to keep client focused

David   Yes, and without that, the whole thing loses meaning because it is this enormous influence from outside that I can't control. They said they found it very difficult to talk about it and welcomed the fact that I had noticed that they looked awful, and my comment was, 'you've got to be blind not to notice how bad you look, but I was shocked to see the difference'. I've been off work for three weeks and the difference in them after three weeks was startling. So why I feel frustrated, is because there are such very major external influences that I don't seem able to help him deal with. However, it all gets mirrored over into their frustration about how the organisation treats them. I just see there are a lot of parallels in their disappointment with perhaps the way that their marriage has turned out and with the way they feel the organisation treats them.

Margaret   You mentioned when you first started talking about it that this wasn't the first time it had happened. Is what you are saying then that each time it has happened, it is directly related to personal circumstances? Each time their performance has dropped, it is directly related to personal circumstances?

Counsellor is recapping what client has said, to link themes and demonstrate listening

David   It seems to be so. When I have challenged their poor performance, and they open up, what they talk about is the fact that they are going through a major difficulty at home. The last time it happened, it was because the divorce papers were about to be served. This time it was because the papers that were being served, have been served and they are trying to get to court to finalise the settlement. Because I don't know exactly what is going on in their personal life the whole time, I can't predict what will happen at work. I just seem to catch it at the bottom the whole time.

167

Margaret   You mentioned that you had challenged him on it: what happened when you challenged him?

Counsellor is focusing the client, trying to establish exactly what the client has said to the individual

David   He agreed that his performance was poor. He told me a lot about his personal life that I did not know, so I understood what the issues were that affected him. He told me a lot about his grievances, about how he felt he had been poorly treated by the company and wasn't recognised for his skills. I spent an hour with him and then said, 'I am happy to see you for another hour to talk about some of the things that have come out, if you feel it would be helpful.'

What happened was that his performance picked up markedly, and about two months later, when we were in the car one day, he said, 'it's the first time anyone has actually noticed that type of thing at work and I want to thank you because it really helped – just to talk about it and to know that someone had noticed'.

At this point in the interview, David is describing the stage he has reached with the client, but this is clearly not the end of the issue ...

Appendix 2

■

Case Study Two:
Annotated counselling session transcript

Session Two: Simon is part way through a session with Katherine, and tries to help her deal with some complex emotions which are affecting her ability to manage, not only a team member, but anyone ...

Simon When you were talking just then, it sounded to me like you were almost reacting like a parent. A child comes to you with a problem and a part of you wanted to solve that problem and help that child, and almost take control from the child of their problem. Like a very caring parent, you wanted to help them and then, what seemed to happen by taking that control, you took away the responsibility from the child. So, when they didn't do anything, when they didn't make the changes you expected from them, you were still in the role of the parent, only this time you were quite angry with them for not doing what you expected them to do.

Counsellor is using emotive images to stir emotions in the client

Katherine I agree with the caring parent bit, like I would like to help. However, I think one thing I have been quite conscious of is saying 'this is your baby – try and sort it out yourself', but perhaps not feeling that I've helped them sort it out. I am quite aware that this is his problem, not mine and that the issues about his career prospects within the company, are him. I have tried to talk to him about potential options and talked about what they might be and I have had quite strong 'no, that's not what I'd like to do' and thought, 'well, OK, that might be what I would think is best for you but you don't see it quite that way and that's your prerogative'. What I do feel frustrated with is feeling I've failed as a manager.

Simon That again comes back to 'not me – I've failed as a manager' but 'me – I've failed as a parent' in being able to care for them. It does sound to me that you know he has got to take this himself, and it is his issue. What you feel to be taking on yourself is your role in all of this; that you have to cope for them and when they say 'well, yes, it's a very good idea, but ...', you keep coming up with the suggestions for them. But for as long as you do that, they don't have to take on responsibility themselves, so it doesn't feel as though it is to do with you not knowing it is their problem. I think that needs to be quite clear. You are very articulate about the way you describe it. The conflict seems to occur in what you feel you should be doing as a manager.

Counsellor is picking up strong emotive words, like 'failed'

Katherine I feel like I am just about to turn my back on him and say, 'sink or swim and it is up to you' and that I have the power to push him under so that he drowns. I find that very difficult to take. The next step to that would mean well, I think you are going to drown and therefore let's see how quickly you can swim to the life-raft.

Simon Can you tell me a bit more about where you would say he was in relation to the life-raft?

Katherine I would think … it's difficult because it is so up and down, it's like being on a stormy sea and that some days, he is certainly in the raft and other days, he is about five miles from it.

Simon And does he know that? Is that something that is explicit between you?

Katherine Um – well, I guess because I hesitate, perhaps it is not. I think where we have talked about what is good and bad, well poor, about his performance, he is clear on the fact that not finishing things on time and the fact that I keep having to ask him for what is going on is not acceptable, and that is five miles from the life-raft. What I know I haven't done is said, 'look, you know, I feel like I am at the end of the road and let's get it quite clear that either you swim for the life-raft' or you just say, 'OK, I'm going to take the life-jacket off'.

Client is becoming confused in their speech. They may be defensive about not confronting the issues

171

Simon Yes, it almost feels as though you hand him a rope to the life-raft and then you turn away and he is left to climb up on that himself without any kind of time frame. In practical terms it sounds like you meet with him and somehow that kind of raises his confidence levels so he is able to function. Then it all slips backwards again but, as I mentioned before, I don't have any sense of you making that explicit to him and I am wondering if that is a missing piece to the relationship; that

Counsellor is bringing the client away from allegory into reality to try to enable the client to accept what they have done

you give him some boundaries, some guidelines and he is left there or he doesn't take them up and then there is no kind of follow up until he falls down again. I didn't explain that very well.

Katherine No, I know what you mean and part of me thinks, 'why the hell should I have to do that for him' and that why can't he do it and sort himself out. Because – and this is quite a strong thing – I do that for myself, so why can't he do that for himself. Because it's bad enough having to do it for me, let alone him. And it's almost like, phew, you know, 'for heaven's sake, you are an adult, aren't you, you know what you need to deliver and when'. Yet I can hear that that is quite contradictory to the bit about, 'look, I really care, but you are all right'.

Client is beginning to voice the true causes of their frustration and resentment

Simon Well, if you take that back to the analogy we were talking about, about parenting, that almost sounds like you have dropped out of your parent role and you are another sibling and you're actually saying, 'oh, look, this is taking an awful lot of my time and no one is looking after me, so just get on with it', because he is not actually doing what you say he should be doing.

Katherine No, I feel that inasmuch as I think well no one does that for me and to keep doing that is not ... that bit is hard work for me.

Simon So, managing him in this particular case means he must respond to your suggestion, then?

Counsellor is trying to focus the client with one question

Katherine   Yes, but I feel quite bad about saying, 'well, sort yourself out' completely.

Simon   That is quite extreme, isn't it? One extreme is, 'go away and sort yourself out' and the other extreme is, 'well, let me take it all on for you'. I am not sure you know where you stand on that continuum.

Katherine   I'm not sure I want to know where I stand on that continuum.

Simon   What do you mean by that?

Katherine   I'm not sure I really, really care.

Simon   About him?

Katherine   Er, no .... deep down, I think, 'well, it's up to you' and that, yes, when we get close and I say, 'tell me what's going on', I do care but, quite frankly, I don't care enough to spend my heart and soul and energy doing it because I've enough on for me to keep me above water. Quite frankly, we're all linked to the life-raft and if you can't swim as quickly as the rest of us, that's tough luck mate.

Simon   That sounds like you perceive your role as an individual and a sibling but if you are this individual's manager, where does that leave you in terms of your responsibility to manage him?

Katherine   Well, that's where I think, 'well, that's not really what it's about' and that is, you know where you catch yourself out and think what I'd really like to say, is 'well, sort yourself out' but my

173

sense of responsibility as a manager is quite strong which is why I take a lot of time to listen to him. But the conflict between 'actually I know my role as a manager is to manage him properly' and, 'I'm not really sure I can be bothered to be a good manager' is enormous, because it drains an enormous amount of energy from me and, as you said, it's the sort of person crying and saying, 'who's doing that for me' – I know and that makes me feel even more awful for thinking 'so why can't I provide that for someone else?'

Simon It sounds to me like we're reaching quite a key point here which is about your perception of what a manager should do and that would seem to create a conflict which I suspect is not only being shown with this guy, but probably been present in other people that you've managed within the team. It feels like you are not sure about what you want from the people you manage. Would that be a correct perception ?

Counsellor summarises and focuses client on key core issue

Katherine I think what I want is not too much trouble from them. I am very clear on that.

Simon And what will you do to them if they 'create trouble'?

Counsellor is using the client's emotive phrase to reflect the framework

Katherine I think what I do or what I feel is I actually feel ... what tends to happen is that I feel I withdraw my support from those who I think – I don't know – create trouble. It is not the right word, say, pull from me in a way that I don't like giving or think, well I don't feel

The confusion in the client's speech reflects the confusion in their mind

that I'm cut out to give in that way or I can be bothered to do. That sounds awful.

Simon Let's stick to what sounds awful, because I am not quite sure I am clear about what 'in that way' means. Could you explain to me what you meant by that?

Counsellor is trying to clear up the confusion by clarifying the client's thoughts

Katherine I don't want to have to have people who work for me who aren't as self-motivated and able to see what is required and deliver as I am because it detracts, it pulls, it takes a lot of my energy to do anything about it. It stops me putting my energy to where *I* get some satisfaction. Whilst I get a lot of satisfaction from saying, 'yes, I've listened to you and I've helped', I can't do that on a regular basis because either I don't notice, I don't make enough time, or I just have got other things I would rather be doing. I just find it such a draw on me that it sort of pulls me down to a base level – or I feel it does – and stops me, as I see it, performing highly in other areas. The conflict is that as a manager I am paid to do that sort of thing, so where does that leave you?

17~~5~~

Client is trying to pass responsibility for any resolution over to the counsellor

Simon It is nothing to do with where it leaves me, it is to do with where it leaves you.

Counsellor passes it back to the client

Katherine Well, that is what I am saying.

Client is still unhappy holding it

Simon So where does it leave you ?

Counsellor repeats question

Katherine Well, it seems to me understanding that there's a fundamental part

of managing other people if they are not high performers that I find extremely difficult and am reluctant to do on a regular basis. I have been thinking about this recently and I think that I am actually best at performing where I can go into a team and make quite a big impact and come out. Whereas where I have got people who are not high performing
and find me stimulating and able to drive them forward – I am not sure that people who are average or poor performers get the same support from me and I find that quite difficult to contend with because it does not fit with my image of being a high performing manager.

Client is beginning to accept and own the real issue for her

Katherine has begun to see where the real issue lies for her, and will need time to reflect on the implications for her ... more work for Simon ...

Appendix 3

■

Personal skills audit

The skills of counselling

The same basic skills are useful in a great range of interviews. Below is a list of skills used by effective interviewers before, during and after the interview as though on a scale of competence, from 1 = weak to 4 = strong. Circle the number which represents where you think you are, in relation to each skill. Then draw a second circle round the three skills you would most like to improve.

Part A – BEFORE THE INTERVIEW

1.	PLANNING	I tend to rely on my general experience to guide me on topics to cover in an interview	1 2 3 4	I think out the purpose and plan of the interview in advance
2.	SETTING THE SCENE	I often have to do with makeshift arrange-ments (room etc.)	1 2 3 4	I always try to set the scene for an interview, prevent interruptions etc.
3.	STAYING OBJECTIVE	I find I do make assumptions before the interview	1 2 3 4	I always try to keep an open mind until I get to know the other person's situation

Part B – DURING THE INTERVIEW

4.	SETTING BOUNDARIES	I think it is up to the other person to make their case. I don't aim to help them	1 2 3 4	I describe how the interview will proceed, and any relevant parameters (e.g. time, subject)
5.	CONTROLLING BIAS (1)	I prefer to interview someone who has a similar background to myself	1 2 3 4	I feel comfortable interviewing all kinds of people

		1	2	3	4	
6. CONTROLLING BIAS (2)	After five minutes or so I usually find I can make up my mind on the issue	1	2	3	4	I aim to build up a good picture before coming to conclusions
7. CONTROLLING BIAS (3)	I do have favourite questions which I think get quickly to the heart of the matter	1	2	3	4	I use a variety of questions in response to the individual
8. CONTROLLING THE OTHER	I have difficulties with both over-talkative and quiet interviewees	1	2	3	4	I can manage to control or encourage the other person as necessary
9. FACING AWKWARD ISSUES	I try to keep off areas which might prove embarrassing to discuss	1	2	3	4	I find I can explore awkward facts without much difficulty
10. LEARNING ABOUT FEELINGS	I think it is often impertinent to ask about a person's feelings	1	2	3	4	I always try to learn about feelings
11. NEUTRAL QUESTIONING	I quite often attack or challenge because I learn a lot from the other person's reactions	1	2	3	4	I try to ask all questions in a friendly, neutral manner
12. OBSERVING	I don't notice much difference in the way people act when I interview them	1	2	3	4	I learn a lot from watching how a person reacts while we talk (e.g. eye gaze, posture)
13. SIGNPOSTING	I find it helpful to spring new topics on people and note their reactions	1	2	3	4	I usually find it helpful to introduce new topics and to explain what I am after
14. SUMMARISING	I would never share my conclusions during an interview	1	2	3	4	I find it helpful to summarise what I am hearing and ask for comments
15. KEEPING TO TIME	I let an interview run as long as it has to	1	2	3	4	I set a specific time for an interview and try to keep to time

Part C – AFTER THE INTERVIEW

		1	2	3	4	
16. FOLLOWING UP	I find I am often too busy to follow up	1	2	3	4	I am careful to follow up on any action agreed

178

The skills of counselling action plan

Review the ratings you gave yourself on The Skills of Counselling Personal Assessment form. Tick all the skills in which you now feel competent, in the Can Do column. Fill in the Improvement Needed column with regard to the others, specifying as precisely as possible what you think you need to practise (e.g. 11. Neutral Questioning: 'Particularly when interviewing people who show off'.) Then in the column Opportunities to Practise, fill in any opportunity you may have, in work or private life, to practise the skill.

Skill	Can do	Improvement needed	Opportunities to practise (Define)
1. PLANNING			
2. SETTING THE SCENE			
3. STAYING OBJECTIVE			
4. SETTING BOUNDARIES			
5. CONTROLLING BIAS (1)			
6. CONTROLLING BIAS (2)			
7. CONTROLLING BIAS (3)			
8. CONTROLLING THE OTHER			
9. FACING AWKWARD ISSUES			
10. LEARNING ABOUT FEELINGS			

Counselling for Change

Skill	Can do	Improvement needed	Opportunities to practise (Define)
11. NEUTRAL QUESTIONS			
12. OBSERVING			
13. SIGN-POSTING			
14. SUMMARISING			
15. KEEPING TO TIME			
16. FOLLOWING UP			

180

Appendix 4

■

Where to get counselling

This is a list of the many organisations that provide a counselling service.

Independent Counselling and
Advisory Services
P O Box 615
Woburn Sands
Milton Keynes NK17 87W
All aspects of counselling

British Association of Counselling
37a Sheep Street
Rugby CV21 3BX
01788 78328
Central information

British Association of
Psychotherapists
121 Hendon Lane
London N3 3P3
0181 346 1747
Referral and assessment services

Alcohol Counselling Services
34 Electric Lane
London SW9 8JT
0171 737 574

Relate
76a New Cavendish Street
London W1M 7LB
0171 580 1087/1088
*Mainly marital but will deal
with other issues*

Alcoholics Anonymous
London Office
11 Redcliffe Gardens
London SW10
0171 352 3001

Information and Social
Services
P O Box 1
Stonebow House
Stonebow
York YO1 2NJ
0904 644020

Release
Criminal, Legal and Drugs Service
169 Commercial Street
London E1
0171 377 9505
0171 603 8654 (24 hr-help line)

Westminster Pastoral Foundation
23 Kensington Square
London W8 5HN
0181 937 6956
*As well as individual and group
counselling, provides service for
organisations called Counselling
in Companies*

SCODA
Standing Conference On Drug
Abuse
1 Hatton Place
London EC1
0171 430 2341

CEPEC
Kent House
41 East Street
Bromley
Kent BR1 1QQ
*Trains in post-incident support
– support for employers in banks,
health service, prisons, police
services, retailing, transport*

Creative Management
Moorlow Tor
Granby Road
Bradwell, Sheffield S30 2HU
01433 621281
*Individual counselling and
executive coaching in organisations
Group and individual supervision
for those providing counselling*

Appendix 5

■

Suggested reading

1. Stress

Causes, Coping and Consequences of stress at Work, Cary L. Cooper and Roy Payne (eds), Wiley, 1988

You don't have to go home from work exhausted, A. McGee-Cooper, Bowen & Rogers, 1990

2. General Management

The Social Psychology of Work, Michael Argyle, Penguin, 1989

Process Consultation, E. Schein, Addison-Wesley, 1988

Managing People at Work: A Manager's Guide to behaviour in Organisations, John Hunt, McGraw Hill, 1993

Healing the wounds, David Noer, Jossey Bass, 1993

3. Counselling Skills

Counselling People at Work: An Introduction for Managers, R. de Board, Gower, 1983

The Skilled Helper, Gerard Egan, Brooks Cole, 1985

Counselling in an Organisation, J. D. Dicken and F. J. Roethlisberger, Harvard University, 1966

Exercises in Helping Skills: A Training Manual to Accompany the Skilled Helper, Gerard Egan, Brooks Cole, 1985

On Becoming a Counseller: A Basic Guide for Non-professional Counsellers, E. Kennedy, Gill and Macmillan, 1977

Principles of Further Counselling, BBC Further Education, London, 1978

Practical Counselling Skills, R. Nelson-Jones, Holt Rinehart and Winston, 1983

You just don't understand, D. Tannen, Ballantine Books, 1990

4. Interpersonal skills

What do you say after you say hello? Eric Berne, Corgi, 1974

Games people play, Eric Berne, Penguin, 1964

Staying OK, A. & T. Harris, Jonathan Cape, 1985

On becoming a person, C. R. Rogers, Constable and Co., 1967

Index

185

187